LEARNING STYLES:

Quiet Revolution in American Secondary Schools

By
Rita Dunn and Shirley A. Griggs

Published by
NATIONAL ASSOCIATION OF SECONDARY SCHOOL PRINCIPALS
1904 Association Drive ● Reston, Virginia

Rita Dunn is professor, Division of Administrative and Instructional Leadership, and director, Center for the Study of Learning and Teaching Styles, St. John's University, New York.

Shirley A. Griggs is professor of counselor education, St. John's University, New York.

Executive Director: Scott D. Thomson
Director of Publications: Thomas F. Koerner
Editors: Carol Bruce
                         Patricia Lucas George
Technical Editor: Eugenia Cooper Potter

National Association of Secondary School Principals
1904 Association Drive, Reston, Virginia 22091
(703) 860-0200

Contents

Foreword

SOME ideas in education are practical, some are not. This monograph provides strong evidence that the application of learning style in a school setting is useful as well as practical. It works for students, it works for teachers, and it works for principals.

Of course, the best way to prove practicality is to observe programs in action. The authors, Professor Rita Dunn and Professor Shirley Griggs of St. John's University, two national leaders in the field of learning style, packed their bags last winter, braved the vicissitudes of airline travel, and visited 10 secondary schools across the nation to observe firsthand classrooms that utilize knowledge of learning style to improve student achievement and build positive attitudes.

Their observations and analysis comprise this monograph. Written informally and interestingly, the authors provide solid testimony to the accomplishments of schools actually integrating learning style into the educational program.

Dunn and Griggs are both experienced teachers as well as university professors. They tell their story well. Their observations and insights will be useful to all schools interested in implementing learning style successfully with students.

Learning style provides important insight into the ways individual students process information to learn. It is a practical professional tool for an increasing number of schools. These schools, in turn, possess a growing reservoir of good advice for other schools.

We urge you to read carefully about the programs described in this publication to see if some advantage may be gained for your students and your school.

Scott D. Thomson
Executive Director
NASSP

Preface

TWO women struggled with the suitcases they had wheeled through the crowded terminal at LaGuardia Airport.

"Why don't you just check these?" asked the security guard at the x-ray luggage machine.

One woman glanced up from her effort to disconnect the baggage carrier cords. "They include our camera, film, batteries, tape recorder, tapes, pads, pens, and travel arrangements. We couldn't function without them!"

"If you two can't travel lighter than this," the guard quipped, "you ought to have some people along to help you!"

And so it began. We realized that with all the baggage of a lifetime that we both carried with us wherever we went, we needed help to decipher the data we had discovered.

We hope that, through this book, you will accompany us on our visits to 10 diversified secondary schools throughout the United States. We observed their learning styles programs and, unexpectedly, found the most exciting ventures into improved instruction that we two veteran educators have ever encountered.

We need you along. We need you to monitor what we saw and to help interpret the findings. We need your objective perceptions.

For, if we are correct, we observed a quiet revolution—one that may influence secondary education for years to come.

Rita Dunn
Shirley A. Griggs

CHAPTER 1

Introduction to Learning Style

MOST PEOPLE DO NOT LIKE CHANGE, and that is understandable. We become comfortable with patterns. They permit us to turn on our automatic functioning mechanism so that we don't have to think.

But we are educators, and many years ago we promised ourselves that we were going to be *good* educators, ones who think and care. But then we came face to face with "the system." The system does not like change any more than people do; in fact, it fights change. The system lulls us into believing that people cannot alter the way it operates. It drones on, day after day, reminding us that it is huge and that it controls countless numbers of non-caring, non-thinking humans—too many to reach and change.

But we are inside the system. We are part of it. If the system is not effective it is important that those of us who are inside it recognize that and do something about it.

The system works well for some, but not for others. Fantini and Weinstein (1968), Holt (1970), and Kohl (1969) understood that certain youngsters could not function well within the system and were alienated by it. As a result, they advocated alternative schools.

Then Martin (1977) examined alternative schools and found that only certain types of students achieved well within them, and that the ones who did were significantly different from the ones who did not.

Raywid (1981) began espousing many different types of alternative schools for the many different types of students in the system, but the system drowned out those suggestions. It was acceptable to assign the trouble-makers and nonconformists who clogged the system's technology to alternative schools, but too many withdrawals would reduce registration and income.

Then it was proposed that a voucher system permit parents to place their youngsters in schools of their choice. By that time, the system had become sophisticated. It challenged the un-Americanism of competing educational institutions; it screamed that it would not survive schools of choice.

Many educational reform reports have examined the system and its outcomes (Fantini, 1986); not one reported what truly is wrong with it.

Curriculum revisions, although necessary, will not improve learning. Neither will expanding academic requirements, beginning education earlier, increasing teachers' salaries, lengthening the school day, providing separate help for the slow learners or the gifted, eliminating tracking, in-

1

creasing expectations, assigning more homework, raising college admission standards, testing for proficiency beyond the classroom, establishing a core curriculum, or revising vocational or work courses.

Of course, those reports were not developed by researchers who also were experienced practitioners and willing to confront the system. Rather, they were developed by intelligent people from many walks of life who sought reasons for poor results. Such groups attain momentary attention and cause legislators to mandate change, but mandates can only have a positive impact on a system when they are directed at the real causes of its failure and are attended to by intelligent, courageous insiders.

In the meantime, it is the rare urban high school whose students are not well below the 50th percentile on nationally normed reading tests; approximately 25 percent of our students have reading problems (Kintsch, 1979). Indeed, as many as 20 percent of all American 17-year-olds were functionally illiterate in 1975 (Lerner, 1981), and those figures do not include people who can, but consistently choose not to, read (Maeroff, 1982). And these data say nothing about how few students like attending school, and how many do so only under stress.

None of this *has* to be. Students *can* function well in school and enjoy it, if we only are willing to examine *how they learn* and redirect the system— *our* system—to respond to their individual instructional needs.

Learning Styles

Link Between Individual Differences and Effective Instruction

Our system is ineffective because it does not respond to the many different ways in which healthy, normal, motivated students absorb, process, and retain difficult information and skills. Although various researchers define the concept differently (Dunn et al., 1981), very few learning style identification instruments are reliable and valid (Curry, 1987).*

No teacher can interpret accurately or extrapolate valid conclusions from data from unreliable and invalid instruments; thus, it is important to become familiar with the three or four that provide trustworthy data.

Regardless of the model, learning styles are unique and different. Everyone has one and, strangely, the styles of husbands and wives and parents and their offspring tend to differ dramatically. Within families, the styles of siblings tend to be more different from each other than similar.

---

*The Curry report is available from St. John's University's Center for the Study of Learning and Teaching Styles, Utopia Parkway, Jamaica, New York 11439, (718) 969-8000 extensions 6335, 6336. In addition, information concerning appropriate instruments is available from either that Center or from the National Association of Secondary School Principals, 1904 Association Drive, Reston, Virginia 22091, (703) 860-0200.

Today, we can test any secondary student and, within minutes, describe exactly how that person is likely to learn more easily and remember longer. We also can explain the methods, resources, and environment likely to best respond to that person's learning style.

What Is Learning Style?

Learning style is a biologically and developmentally imposed set of characteristics that make the same teaching method wonderful for some and terrible for others.

It describes the way a classroom would be organized to respond to individual needs for quiet or noise, bright or soft illumination, temperature differences, seating arrangements, mobility needs, or grouping preferences. It suggests the patterns in which people tend to concentrate best—alone, with others, with certain types of teachers, or in a combination thereof. It suggests the senses through which people tend to remember difficult information most easily—by hearing, speaking, seeing, manipulating, writing or notetaking, experiencing, or, again, a combination of these.

Learning style also considers motivation, on-task persistence, or the need for multiple assignments simultaneously, the kind and amount of structure required, and conformity versus nonconformity levels.

Chronobiology is also part of style. Some people cannot function well at the same time of day during which others are at their best. And, although only one instrument considers individual needs for eating or drinking while concentrating, intake achieved the highest reliability when a National Association of Secondary School Principals (NASSP) Task Force examined all the characteristics that tend to have an impact on student achievement.

Responsiveness to these variables triggers students' concentration and gets them ready to learn. How they actually process the information they need to master is called their hemisphericity; some people refer to hemisphericity as left/right, others call it analytic/global, inductive/deductive, reflective/impulsive, and so forth. They are referring to that component of learning style that educational psychologists call cognitive style.

Extensive research documents that statistically higher test scores, improved attitudes toward school and learning, and reduced number of discipline problems result when students are taught through their personal learning style strengths (see Appendices). Research from more than 40 graduate institutions of higher education in the United States verifies the differences that exist among students; and many well-conducted, experimental studies demonstrate how well the same youngsters learn when they are taught correctly (for them) and how poorly they learn when they are taught through methods that do not complement their styles.

Misconceptions about how learning occurs are what caused the system to break down in the first place. As long as schools graduated the students whose styles responded to the system and cast out, permitted to drop out, or relegated to nonacademic training those whose styles found the system unresponsive, citizens believed in it. But once they were asked to educate all youngsters and keep them in school beyond 16, and we, and they, found that the system could not do that, researchers began to wonder why. It was then that we began to understand individual learning styles.

Most people may not like change, but some recognize the need to change the system. It may not be easy to reprogram a bureaucracy, but some outstanding administrators and teachers have been doing just that. Within their own secondary schools, they have accosted many of the things that made the system inefficient and have combated deep-seated prejudices and misconceptions about learning held by the public and boards of education.

These educators are the pioneers of our decade. They are the instructional leaders of American secondary schools. They have operated out of concern, conviction, and contempt for the notion that the system cannot be changed. These people have changed it in their schools. They have redesigned instruction to respond to students' diversified learning styles.

CHAPTER 2

Midwest High School —A Small Public School in Rural Wyoming

Box 368
Midwest, Wyo. 82643
Contact Person: Jeff Jacobson, Principal
(307) 437-6571

T HE POVERTY OF THIS ONCE-THRIVING AMOCO company town is apparent by its boarded-up businesses and its many empty houses. A post office, a mini-mart, and a local clinic staffed two half-days a week are the only services remaining other than the K-12 school system.

Midwest's sober economy—an outgrowth of declining oil prices and widespread layoffs—has had an impact on the area in many ways. When people could no longer earn a living in the area they moved away, resulting in business closings. Homes were sold at a fraction of their original cost; recreation facilities were limited to the next town's two bars, bowling alley, and restaurant.

Midwest High School brightens the lives of its 130 students in grades 7-12 and their families. In 1983, Jeff Jacobson became principal. His plan was to revitalize the educational program so it would nurture the community's young people on a full-day basis.

At that time, the high school's curriculum reflected the restrictiveness of a faculty limited to only 18 teachers. To increase student attendance and motivation, faculty members were asked to broaden their repertoire of course offerings to include high-interest subjects and topics or skills that might be scheduled on either a short or long-term basis. Additions included everything from esoteric art projects to gourmet cooking, to Indian warhead and other relic searches, to varied sports activities, to music and drama. With the teachers' five preparations per day, these add-ons routinely required faculty participation in late afternoon and evening activities.

During his first year, Jacobson described some of the area's problems in a proposal he submitted to the Carnegie Foundation. For example, because only about 30 percent of the parents had completed high school, student aspirations rarely included a four-year college education; a few applied for admission into community colleges, but 75 percent or more sought employment immediately after high school.

Jacobson's request to the Carnegie Foundation was for training in learning styles—a concept he thought might help more faculty members reach more students.

Concomitant with his application, the school was transformed into a community center; classes were conducted during the day and recreational activities and interesting courses, seminars, clubs, and other activities were available in the afternoon and evenings. Teachers served double and sometimes triple duty as instructors, coaches, class advisers, special events leaders, and so forth.

To attract teachers willing to devote their fullest measure of dedication and time, the school board renovated 19 homes and made them available to faculty members for less than $90 per month rent. It also paid moderate stipends for the additional after-school duties.

Because it was deemed crucial to provide students with many positive recreational activities and to develop community pride, coaches were well-paid. A strong parent-student community focus was emphasized.

When Midwest High School's proposal was awarded a Carnegie Foundation grant, Jacobson reviewed various learning style models, collected published materials to share with his faculty, and decided to learn about using instruction based on learning styles himself.

The Role of Administration

In 1984, Jacobson attended a one-week learning styles workshop in New York. He returned to his high school and met with faculty members to explain learning styles theory and concept. He then tested the teachers for their learning styles. A few weeks later, he distributed their individual profiles, interpreted the information, and asked for volunteers to meet with him periodically to learn more about teaching students through their identified strengths.

Of the 18 faculty members, teachers in English, mathematics, reading, home economics, French, and art volunteered—8 in all. The resource room specialist and the secondary level counselor also chose to participate.

Periodically, Jacobson and the eight volunteers met, shared information, and developed instructional materials. They administered an instrument to identify their students' styles, examined the profiles, and experimented with several beginning techniques.

One year later, Jacobson received additional training, and during the second year of the program's implementation, he continued to meet with teachers to expand their expertise. In 1987, Jacobson and one of his most interested faculty members attended an advanced leadership institute on learning styles.

Observations

In sharp contrast to its dull, rocky, arid geographical surroundings, Midwest High School's interior is an explosion of bright color, student art, and attractive posters. Every door boasts the subject and the teacher's name on an attractive sign. Credit for this highly attractive environment is due largely to the creative skills of Bryce Cool, Midwest's art teacher. He uses learning style visuals about art to help students develop artistic talents.

Several classrooms, including that of reading teacher Marty Gotschall, have redesigned environments, permitting those who require a quiet area to work informally. This informal environment is also present in the library-media center, where Sherry Good allows students to use bean bag and support furniture as they work or read. Most classrooms have conventional desks and seats but when students relax and stretch, no one admonishes them. Individuals who stand for a moment to change positions are not considered disruptive.

Most classes encourage varied groupings. Thus, students completing identical assignments may work alone, in pairs, or in small groups. When additional information is required, students ask the teacher, who circulates among them.

Two teachers have translated a few of their curriculum units into complementary resources. Thus, a few pupils were learning about mythology with a Contract Activity Package, while others used a Programmed Learning Sequence, and a larger group worked directly with the teacher.

The consumer math teacher, Bryan Balfour, introduced a unit on how to purchase a car by urging the individuals to select the vehicle of their choice. He provided current references that evaluated the various models and served as price guides. A script was distributed wherein salespeople tried to sell potential purchasers other cars or the same model at different prices with high-pressure tactics.

Role playing put the situation into perspective, but teamwork permitted group analysis of the techniques employed by salespeople, purchasers, and managers. This introductory instruction was supplemented by a small-group technique, Team Learning, during the next period.

While requesting students' responses to math problems, Bob Cochran asked how each had reached the answer. He encouraged alternative thinking and processing; when students provided those he pursued their thinking strategies. When no one could think of different ways of doing the problems, he described some.

Cochran consistently probed their problem-solving patterns and encouraged diversified ways of attacking tasks. He also encouraged students to translate the words into graphic symbols—a highly global technique for math, which often is taught analytically (step by step, building up to comprehension rather than through application that gradually leads to the details).

The resource room teacher circulated among those youngsters who were experiencing difficulty with one or more academic subjects. She patiently taught study skills for analyzing the important ideas in passages, recording them, and applying them.

Each student needed different kinds of assistance and, as she moved from one to the other, she would ask, "What don't you understand?" or "Where's the trouble?" followed by "What's your learning style strength?" She then guided students toward comprehension using the youngsters' styles to determine the approach.

Everywhere, students interacted with each other or the teacher according to their preferences. In every class, a few isolated themselves from others, sometimes behind dividers and often with earplugs to block out sound. Students spoke softly, politely, and in a controlled, adult manner.

As we walked through the school unattended, in classes, in corridors, in lunch rooms, in recreational facilities, and in the library, we asked students about their feelings toward school, their teachers, their classes, and learning. Unlike those of many secondary students, their responses were universally laudatory. These adolescents liked being in school, recognized its favorable influence on their lives, and appreciated their teachers' efforts on their behalf.

Gale Upchurch serves as the district guidance counselor. In only her third year, she is enthusiastic about the learning styles approach for youth. She strives to match counseling interventions (individual, peer, or group) to students' preferences, and works with students to develop study habits that are congruent with their styles.

A sustained reading program was in effect throughout the school. At 10:15 every morning, all students, teachers, staff members, and Jacobson stopped whatever they were doing and read whatever they wanted as long as it would be considered appropriate for inclusion in the school library.

The secondary resource classroom reflected the individual assignments made by Susan Minotti, the resource teacher. Minotti differentiates between individualization and learning style, perceiving that the former permits students to learn at their own *rate;* the latter to learn in their own *way.*

She credits her learning style responsiveness for the number of pupils who voluntarily come to her and say, "I'm having trouble in _____; may I work here?" They seat themselves in whichever position they feel most comfortable, wherever in the room they like to concentrate, and then just get to work.

Minotti insisted that the learning style environment, and aid when they need it, empowers many of these youngsters to function better than they previously had in traditional classrooms.

Terri Brantz, the English teacher, used colored wooden blocks to help students learn the parts of speech tactually. She provided descriptive cards to indicate the patterns of required sentences, and small groups of students, using blocks, then created their own sentences following the specific patterns designated on the board.

For example, Brantz would instruct students to "Develop a sentence in the following format: adjective, noun, conjunction, adjective, noun, verb, adverb, preposition, article, noun." Students might create a sentence such as "Pretty Susan and handsome John ran swiftly down the street." Then they would place the colored blocks matching each part of speech beneath the corresponding words.

The tactual manipulation of the blocks supplemented the thinking and writing and enhanced the learning experience. By permitting students to work in teams if they preferred to do so, Brantz reduced their anxiety and facilitated cooperative interactions.

Conclusions and Recommendations

Despite the fact that Midwest High School's teachers have five classes daily and two to three cocurricular activities for which they are responsible, they show positive attitudes toward teaching through learning style strengths, responding to student differences, and gradually expanding their repertoire of teaching techniques to match youngsters' styles.

The school has adopted alternative schedules, permitting the core curriculum to be taught in the morning one week and in the afternoon the next, to avoid favoring only one chronobiological time preference.

The average number of absences per year decreased significantly after learning styles instruction was initiated, and overall achievement gains reflect that 73 percent of students are now on grade level or higher as measured by the Stanford Achievement Test.

Furthermore, Midwest students have won 27 of the total 127 Wyoming Congressional Achievement Awards presented during the first four years of the program. Of even more consequence, in a depression area where nearly 70 percent of the parents never completed high school, the dropout rate was reduced to only two in 1986.

CHAPTER 3

Corsicana High School— A Large Public School in A Small Texas Town

West Highway 22
Corsicana, Texas 75110
Contact Person: T. Y. Harp, Principal
(214) 874-8211

T HE YOUNG PEOPLE ATTENDING Corsicana High School attracted attention initially by their energy, movement, direction, and stature, and won visitors completely once they began to converse. Personality and candor, combined with a genuine interest in others typified the many conversations during our two days in the school. One student's observation was as follows:

> A long time ago (prior to 1978) many students complained that teachers were prejudiced against blacks and Mexicans. Then Dr. Harp became principal. He made it clear that anyone who did not like teaching children—*all children*—was not welcome here. Some people left. Now there are lots of different kinds of teachers here, but they all like all of us .... They really care about us.

Role of Administration

Corsicana High School, located in a small town 50 miles south of Dallas, has implemented a learning styles approach to instruction primarily through the efforts of its principal, T. Y. Harp, a dynamic, charismatic, and highly credible administrator. Harp humorously refers to himself as a "benevolent despot"; his faculty members more accurately perceive him as a sensitive, understanding, committed leader who commands the respect and trust of teachers and students alike.

Harp has so thoroughly embraced learning styles that he has changed his administrative style, saying the model has helped him better understand situations and made him more confident in handling faculty problems and assignments. He perceives problems more as a conflict between styles than a conflict of personalities.

An NASSP national convention provided Harp's introduction to the learning styles model. Impressed with the research that supported the approach and convinced that learning styles was the vehicle for Corsicana High

School to use to improve academic achievement and decrease student apathy and dropouts, he attended institutes to learn about methods and procedures for initiating change.

Subsequently, he asked teachers to volunteer to work with learning styles, and approximately 30 expressed an interest. Because the volunteers were asked to attend workshops and participate in the number of inservice activities without compensation, the teachers who persisted in the project were among the more dedicated and enthusiastic.

Initially, many teachers were concerned that they would lose control of their classes if they permitted students to sit informally or work with peers to complete tasks. Others were overwhelmed at the prospect of accommodating a variety of learning styles simultaneously. Harp encouraged teachers to experiment with one or two beginning approaches as a means of determining the effectiveness of teaching to student strengths.

To her amazement, a resource teacher who was experiencing serious classroom discipline problems prior to adopting a learning styles approach and was considering leaving the teaching profession found that student behavior improved.

The teachers who have embraced learning styles have become an elite group within the school, and they frequently seek each other out at monthly meetings and other occasions to share techniques, demonstrate small-group procedures, and develop case studies of students who have been thriving as a result of the changes.

Funds for inservice education and student assessment have been limited; however, the principal was able to use monies from vending machine profits and other projects to support these activities.

Homogeneous groupings within the school include extended or enriched, college preparatory, and basic-skills classes. Teachers work with all three groups within a discipline. At first the teachers thought that basic-skills students would be most amenable to learning styles approaches. However, they found that high achieving students in the extended classes were equally as enthusiastic about the changes initiated as a result of accommodating their individual instructional preferences.

Gifted students in geometry classes have developed creative materials for use by tactual students. One example is a Bingo game that utilizes geometric concepts and theorems in problem solving.

The principal encourages teachers to share ideas and materials at monthly inservice meetings. Fortunately, there is continuity at the high school; Harp has headed the school since 1978, and the faculty has experienced minimal attrition.

Observations

Between one-third and one-fourth of Corsicana's 86 teachers have become involved to some extent in using students' learning styles as the basis for instructional decisions; only 10 use that information on a daily basis.

All freshman students were tested in September 1986, and their learning style profiles were shared with them and then placed into their cumulative records. As a result, whenever we asked ninth graders what they knew about how they learned, almost all specifically described their preferences, how they had been taught to use their strengths when studying, and how certain teachers had tried to accommodate their differences.

Students' attitudes toward their teachers' efforts to respond to their learning style preferences were consistently laudatory; most feel as if they have been accorded special consideration by an extremely caring faculty.

Teacher Sherrye Dotson reported that one day, when she was ill, one of her math students entered class and automatically walked to the carpeted floor area where Dotson permitted youngsters who worked better informally to do their assignments. The substitute for that day immediately reprimanded the teenager for not seating herself at a desk.

The student quietly rose from the floor and dutifully sat down in a vacant chair. Dotson later asked the student why she didn't explain to the sub that she was permitted to sit in the lounge area. The student laughed and conspiratorially responded, "I didn't want to get you in trouble!"

Dotson also confided that, prior to the advent of her learning styles program, students would wait in the hall until the last minute before classes began. "Now they come into the room, take their books and materials to wherever they feel most comfortable, and immediately get to work. When I start the lesson, they merely stop what they're doing and begin to interact with me."

To corroborate the students' appreciation of their teachers' efforts to work with learning styles, another teacher told us that when she advised her class that Harp would be evaluating her lesson the next day, the youngsters asked, "Do you want us to sit in our chairs when the principal is here?" She was particularly warmed when, during the lesson, a student slipped her a note that said, "You're doing fine!"

We visited Sherrye Dotson's Algebra II class and noted that whenever the teacher talked, she simultaneously graphed, wrote words, or illustrated the permutations she was explaining. Dotson later revealed that many of her students "made better sense of concepts" when they could see, rather than merely hear about what she was describing.

At the end of the 1986-87 school year, she also noted that the solely tactual students who previously had performed poorly in math, had become among the highest algebra achievers during the spring semester. She attributed that outcome to her requirement that the tactual youngsters write and graph their work on a daily basis.

Dotson, who had been a skeptical volunteer in the beginning of the program, became one of its strongest advocates by the end of only one year. She said she had never realized how much capitalizing on individuals' perceptual strengths could affect their math test scores.

In accordance with her belief that when students are required to apply new information in a creative way they remember it better, Dotson assigns homework tasks that yield many original tactual/visual and sometimes kinesthetic games which are then made available as instructional resources to students whose styles are complemented by them.

For example, four eleventh graders jointly designed the Clue Game for a unit on graphing linear equations. As its name suggests, the game provides clues with lines to plot. As the lines or points are graphed, the quadrant into which they fall provides the answers to stories in which people, weapons, or conclusions are missing. Thus, both mysteries and curiosity are satisfied as students use the game to gain experience with assigned math problems.

The creative writing teacher, Lana Orsak, redesigned her classroom to permit her juniors and seniors to study while relaxed in a carpeted, informal area. In addition, she uses small-group instructional techniques such as Team Learning to introduce new, difficult material; Circle of Knowledge to reinforce it; and Brainstorming to foster creativity. She also permits students to snack on raw vegetables or fruits, provided they adhere to regulations she established.

Orsak confirmed that the youngsters adjusted to the changes quickly, their achievement had improved, and she had no behavior problems.

Twelfth grader Bobby Spears reiterated how much easier it was for him to learn through his learning style than through traditional methods. He said that this was his first experience in a relaxed atmosphere, and that permission to use his Walkman to block out extraneous classroom sounds had resulted in the best writing he had ever produced.

We stopped students in halls, classrooms, and outside the building and tape-recorded their answers to the following questions:

- Did they know their own learning style?
- Did it work?
- Did they like learning that way? Why? Why not?

Sondra Flores said that since Orsak had permitted her to work in ways she felt most comfortable (on carpeted floor and with a peer), she "had the highest grades I've ever had."

Stephen Barries, a student from France, commented on the difference between his creative writing learning styles class and instruction in his native country, saying that the Corsicana approach "gives the class a family-like feeling rather than a competitive structure."

Many youngsters reiterated that they learned more effectively through peer-oriented Team Learning and Circle of Knowledge than through conventional lectures or readings—statements confirmed repeatedly by Orsak. Originally she had used those strategies for basic teaching; later she introduced the writing of dialog and poetry that way and found student reactions were positive and enthusiastic. She reported that once youngsters had learned to produce creative writing with their peers, they gradually learned to do the same confidently by themselves.

On the other hand, she said, many capable students were frustrated by the group process; they preferred to complete the task immediately rather than spend time discussing strategies. Apparently, just as some students thrive in traditional classes where others fail, some learn easily and confidently with their peers and have difficulty with teacher-directed instruction.

Orsak said that the small-group techniques permit the peer-motivated students to learn with a relatively relaxed approach.

Senior Eric Middleton said, "I'm really bored in other classes where I am required to learn in exactly the way each teacher plans. Some can adjust; some can't. I can, but I don't enjoy being there. In here, Mrs. Orsak tells us what we must learn and then lets us do it in the way we choose. That makes it easier to study and to learn. It works so well, I've been doing my homework for other classes through my style. But being in those classes is boring."

Molly Sparks, another teacher involved in the learning styles program, would like to provide students with enough alternative materials to permit them to choose how they master required objectives, but during her first year, she decided to teach a part of each lesson auditorially, visually, tactually, and kinesthetically so that each youngster could have multiple experiences, at least one of which would be through his or her preference.

Thus, she first read *Oedipus Rex* into a tape recorder. Auditory youngsters who found reading the novel difficult could listen to the tape as they read along with it. Authority-oriented or teacher-motivated students could read along with Sparks as she read to them. Peer-motivated students could read together and cooperatively develop answers. Visual, self-motivated youngsters could read without listening to the cassette.

Sparks also had made a series of cardboard strips, each of which had various incidents printed on it. After the youngsters had read or heard *Oedipus Rex,* she assigned them to teams of four or five, gave each team a set of the cardboard strips, and challenged them to place the strips into the story's correct sequence of events.

When they had completed that task, Sparks requested volunteers to dramatize the play. To culminate the lesson, she distributed a crossword puzzle on *Oedipus Rex* and encouraged the youngsters to test themselves on the content—either alone, in pairs, or in a team.

For homework, she required the students to use all the information in the crossword puzzle in a creative way. Thus, students could develop a game, poster, book cover, poem, or drawing that included the information.

The variety of activities in the single lesson kept the pace rapid; the type of strategies responded to multiple styles and permitted youngsters to learn as they felt most comfortable sociologically—alone, with peers, or with the teacher. The four who preferred sitting informally sat in the carpeted section; all others remained in their chairs and merely moved them so that they either could work by themselves or with others.

In one home economics room the teacher had printed directions for making a pattern on each sewing machine. She permitted students to follow her recommendations as they preferred. Thus, some read the directions quietly and proceeded step-by-step to work them out. Others asked a class-mate to read the steps as they followed sequentially by hearing and then trying to operate the mechanism. A few barely glanced at the directions, quickly sat down, and tried to learn by doing.

Anecdotes shared by teachers and students clarify some of the management strategies Corsicana faculty members use.

- Lisa Price, an eleventh grader, marched into Lana Orsak's room and asked "When are you gonna teach another learning styles unit?" She'd passed each topic Orsak had converted to allow for individual differences and failed the ones Orsak hadn't had time to translate. When we asked how students knew which strategies or resources to use, Orsak said, "We tell them what their learning styles are and how to use their strengths to learn new and difficult information or skills. Students then choose the best ways for them to learn."
- Sherrye Dotson tells the story of the Algebra student who told her he had increased his test scores by 20 points on every learning styles unit he had done. He attributed those gains to the reduction of pressure and being able to learn in small groups with peers through Team Learning. Prior to Dotson's learning styles program he had twice repeated math courses during summer session.
- Two teachers expressed concern over the labeling of "learning disabled" students. Orsak in particular said that many such youngsters performed well in her classes when they were permitted to learn in their style rather than their teachers'.
- Dorothy Vacek's assignment for a Housing and Home Furnishings unit had been for students to either draw or write a song or poem about their dream closet, one that afforded maximum storage room. Two unbelievably talented youngsters whose drawings exemplified artistic excellence described their personal feelings about this home economics class that permitted them to use their strengths. One said art was the one area in which she felt confident and being able to use that talent in academic courses gave her a chance to excel. The other described a difficult teenage period when the only place he felt "good" was in his learning styles classes.

Conclusions and Recommendations

Corsicana High School is in its second year of learning styles implementation, with approximately half the faculty committed to the model and continuing to pursue inservice education on a regular basis.

Students are highly motivated to achieve academically, and many expressed the belief that learning styles self-awareness enabled them to obtain the grade point average that made them eligible for scholarships.

The administration and faculty are committed to evaluating the impact of the change. The assistant principal charts teacher referrals for disciplinary action weekly and has found a significant reduction of referrals since the onset of the program.

Faculty members who have moved from traditional modes of instruction to a learning styles approach recognize that the greatest changes affect teachers in terms of different attitudes and philosophy, and they embrace the position, "If students cannot learn the way we teach them, we must teach them the way they learn!"

Teachers have studied the commonality among students' learning styles as well as the differences. When assessing the preferred modalities of 196 students, they found that tactual/kinesthetic preferences were prevalent among 40 percent of the students, followed by auditory preferences (31%), and visual preferences (13%). These findings have resulted in the development of a variety of tactual/kinesthetic materials in a broad range of content areas.

Both the administration and faculty share a common commitment to continue learning-styles-based instruction. Each year, increasing numbers of teachers are trained at summer institutes and this core returns to the school to conduct monthly inservice meetings and demonstrations for other teachers.

Those faculty members who are most proficient in this methodology serve as resources for others, who are motivated to change their instructional strategies because of the student benefits they observe.

CHAPTER 4

Sacred Heart Seminary— A Small New York Parochial School

95 Fulton Avenue
Hempstead, N.Y. 11550
Contact Person: Sister Mary Cecilia Giannitti, C.S.J., Principal
(516) 483-2866

I N 1873, THE YEAR OF THE FIRST PENNY postcard, 8 years after the Civil War ended, 3 years before Thomas Edison created the telephone, and 30 years before the Wright brothers made their airplane fly, the railroad was bringing dreamers, realists, risk takers, and cautious entrepreneurs west. In New York, population growth was expanding outward from Manhattan toward Long Island.

Caring deeply for the welfare of the Island's increasing Catholic population, the Sisters of St. Joseph, a service-oriented order, founded schools, hospitals, and orphanages throughout the Brooklyn Diocese, which then encompassed all of Long Island. One of the schools was Sacred Heart Seminary.

The seminary's alcoves, large windows, spacious rooms, covered portico, and winding wooden staircase are exquisite testimony to the elegance of days past. In sharp contrast is its research-based instructional program.

Responsive to the emotional and psychological characteristics of children between the ages of 12 and 14, Sacred Heart teachers analyze the individual needs of each entering youngster and design a unique instructional program for each one.

Based on a combined philosophy of learning-styles-based instruction superimposed onto mastery learning, this school provides an ideal environment for its 121 students from various socioeconomic and achievement levels. The school is small: It includes an elementary division, and a middle school population made up of seven faculty members, who also serve as counselors, and 54 students in grades 6-8.

Visitors' initial reactions center around the picturesque facility, the ideal number of students per class—and the apparently ideal environment in which to individualize instruction.

We must confront that misconception. The youngsters attending this school are bused in from 34 separate districts, and many are the offspring of military personnel and transient professionals. Many students had failed in their former schools; they come from intact, divorced, or separated families; both parents may work; and many share a single-parent environment barely above the national poverty level.

Ten years ago, when Sister Mary Cecilia first became principal, Sacred Heart Seminary was "a traditionally organized school with a dull learning environment." Most of the students seemed bored and uninterested in learning. As a result, frequent discipline problems arose, particularly at the upper grade levels.

Sister Mary encouraged the teachers to move away from lock-step procedures and to individualize students' activities based on their interests and academic needs. Few faculty members supported that concept and, at the end of that first year, many resigned. Sister then employed new instructors more in accord with her intentions to revise instruction.

During the second year, Sister trained teachers to use behavioral objectives, more audiovisual resources, and instructional television. During that period, Sister Mary's graduate studies exposed her to individualization through learning styles. She saw the value of capitalizing on students' strengths and that concept became the foundation upon which teaching and learning at Sacred Heart Seminary is based.

To this day, parents often register their children at Sacred Heart as a last resort; their offspring either have failed or been unhappy at their previous schools. Initially, these students exemplify the typical frustrations of at-risk or dropout students; they are either aggressive or withdrawn, boisterous or noncommunicative, nonconforming or automatonistic.

Sister Mary, who gives awards to students for "being caught doing something good," credits her instructional program and the teachers who implement it for the transformation of frequently-troubled discipline cases to what visitors perceive as "handpicked, dutiful students."

Role of Administration

Sister Mary has been principal since 1977, and cites her major achievement as the implementation of mastery learning and learning-styles-based instruction throughout the school. She initiated these changes by variations in room design, encouraging teachers to introduce teamed activities within each unit of study, and conducting faculty meetings to introduce the concept of individualization.

In 1981, students in each grade of the middle school were assessed to determine their learning style preferences, and parents were invited to group sessions in which the results were explained in relation to different teaching techniques.

Sacred Heart Seminary's climate is marked by productivity and a seriousness of purpose. There are no bells that signal the end of classes; instead, students move to the next class expeditiously. Their appearance and behavior suggest professionalism.

Every attempt is made to accommodate students' preferred time of day through flexible scheduling and rotation of classes by cycle so that all courses are taught at some time during students' peak energy periods. For example, eighth graders are allowed to select their preferred time of day for taking the standardized achievement test.

Focused learning style programs are not available within the high school, but the principal comments, "At that point our students are highly cognizant of their style strengths and are able to make the necessary adaptations within the classroom and outside in terms of study habits. Additionally, at that stage their auditory skills are better developed, enabling them to cope more than previously with lectures."

Overall, the faculty members are very supportive of the principal and perceive her as a competent and effective leader. Typical comments are represented in eighth grade mathematics teacher Rudy Brehler's observations:

> I was hired by Sister on July 14, 1983—that is the date for commemorating Bastille Day in France—and it proved to be a revolution in my life as well. Up to that point, I had taught for eight years in the public schools and I was pretty well burned-out. I had thought about giving up teaching as a career but thought that I would try once more in a different school. During the interview, Sister described the school environment and goals and I became very excited. I love teaching here, because I can really teach!

Other faculty members described the principal as an informed instructional leader who works closely with teachers and encourages team decision making and consensus when implementing change.

Observations

Sacred Heart Seminary reflects the educational beliefs of its principal, who strongly embraces responsiveness to individual characteristics. For example, Sister Mary believes that students' concentration is triggered when they are permitted to learn in a physical environment conducive to their ability to do their best. Thus, every classroom has both traditional seats and desks and an informal, carpeted area.

Sister Mary said that this transformation of a totally conventional school setting into one that at least partially suggested a type of seating permissiveness was not easy for her to adopt. Had she not been fortified by prize-winning research and her own desperation, she doesn't believe she would have experimented with redesigning the school's environment. However, once she encouraged her faculty members to permit certain youngsters to try learning informally, she found that many of her students with the worst discipline problems began to pay better attention and to behave better.

That outcome resulted in her encouraging the seminary's teachers to further experiment by grouping students for instruction on the basis of their sociological preferences.

When Sister introduced small-group strategies to her staff members eight or nine years ago, all had taught essentially through lecture and discussion. Both the principal and her teachers anticipated the worst, for many of their students had consistently been admonished for not sitting erectly, quietly, cooperatively, or attentively.

As the teachers' repertoire expanded to include student-centered techniques for cooperative learning and reinforcing information, faculty members became aware of how much better the adolescents were learning, participating in class activities, and scoring on tests. As a result, during the past several years teachers continue to teach with peer-oriented approaches and new faculty members are indoctrinated as a condition of employment.

Whenever we questioned why they were working in different ways to accomplish identical objectives, students immediately explained that each had a different style and learned more or less easily through specific methods. One of the most impressive attributes of Sacred Heart Seminary's program was that all students had been tested to identify their individual styles and all could describe their strengths and how to best use them to learn.

Sister Mary had also read the research documenting the importance of initially teaching each person new or difficult knowledge through his or her perceptual strengths and reinforcing that information through secondary and tertiary modalities. Thus, each lesson we observed, and the walls of every classroom, reflected the multisensory resources available for mastering each objective.

Furthermore, the value of *applying* newly gained information in a creative way also impressed this principal. Thus, the entire school reflected students' original games, charts, stories, books, poetry, and other projects.

The effects of chronobiology also made an impression on Sister Mary. She became acquainted with the work of other principals who had experimented successfully with matching time-of-day energy highs with both instruction and test administrations. Sacred Heart, therefore, adopted an eight-day time frame that alternates classes in a cycle, enabling each youngster to attend basic courses at their best time of day at least some of the time.

In 1986-87, the seminary administered the Iowa Test of Basic Skills to all its students in two different time frames—early morning and afternoon. Morning preferents took the test then, and afternoon high-energy youngsters attended the afternoon administration.

Eighty-five percent of the seminary's middle school students achieved at the middle of the tenth grade level (10.5)—at a time when other diocesan students' overall scores were decreasing.

Analysis of the most recent tests the diocese administered indicated a stronger emphasis than ever before on critical-thinking and problem-solving skills. The curriculum widely used in the Rockville Centre diocesan schools, at least until recently, was heavily fact/rote-memory oriented, accounting, at least in part, for the gradually decreasing test scores.

Although Sacred Heart's curriculum also emphasizes data retention, the inference and critical thinking questions required in Team Learning exercises (Carbo, Dunn, and Dunn, 1986; Dunn and Dunn, 1978) provide frequent experiences with higher level cognitive skills.

When Sister Mary began the school's learning styles program, each teacher was required to design at least one unit responsive to diversified styles. During the past few years, many faculty members have developed a series of such packages.

The school philosophy includes permitting students who demonstrate trustworthiness to structure at least part of their own time. An unassigned period becomes a privilege afforded to deserving students, an interval during which they may work in the computer or science labs or on creative projects by themselves or with similarly rewarded peers.

Understanding the learning style differences that exist among people, this school permits individuals to function through their strengths. Thus, when youngsters are self-structured and responsible, they are encouraged to extend their activities into self-selected areas; when they require external structure and supervision, their programs reflect directed tasks.

Students quickly learn how to behave responsibly to obtain the privilege of being independent during selected periods of the day. Some have more difficulty than others but faculty members often have been surprised by the rapidity with which seemingly undisciplined teenagers respond to being treated like young ladies and gentlemen.

In part, students' attitudes reflect the appreciation they feel for the seminary's efforts to help them achieve. We interviewed youngsters at random (and without faculty members present) and were told many heart-warming things:

- In public school I just learned information. In this school, I learn information and I learn how to learn . . . .
- Sister believes it is her mission to help us all learn how to teach ourselves!
- Once Sister brought a real skull to class to show us left and right processing styles. I'll never forget that! I like bright light, a desk, quiet, and no intake when learning. I'm a "left," but my mom is the opposite!
- I like this school because it gives us many opportunities to learn in different ways. It's not boring like other schools.
- Can you imagine anyone wanting to learn these things by reading a book? It's so much more fun with this board game and with your friend!

One might suspect that students would enjoy learning through diversified resources and experiences, but the Sacred Heart teachers, who must have contributed endless hours of their time and effort, are also uniformly positive about the program.

Conclusions and Recommendations

The middle school within Sacred Heart Seminary represents a small, private, religious-affiliated school in its ninth year of implementing a learning style approach to instruction.

The principal has completed her tenth year at the Seminary and, through a combination of inservice education and teacher selection based on flexibility and openness to adapting learning style based instruction, she has been able to fully provide for students' individual preferences in most affective, physiological, and cognitive dimensions. Because the administrative structure is uncomplicated, Sister Mary Cecilia can spend time in the classrooms to supervise and support faculty efforts.

Many educators would view this school as an ideal setting. Students are scheduled in learning groups of approximately 8 students; no group exceeds 12. Youngsters are highly motivated and although seminary faculty member salaries are not competitive with those of public schools, there is a low degree of teacher turnover.

Since the entire school is committed to a learning styles approach, there has been minimum attention to evaluating the impact of instruction in the absence of controlled conditions. The principal's perceptions of improvement are subjective, but she has observed positive changes in students' academic achievement and attitudes toward school over the past 10 years.

On the Iowa Test of Educational Achievement the mean language arts scores for students in the middle school changed from 8.5 in 1985/86 to 10.5 in 1986/87. However, with small numbers of students enrolled and tested, it must be recognized that significant improvement in a few students can affect the entire group.

In summary, a number of factors contribute to an outstanding educational experience within Sacred Heart Seminary Middle School. The learning styles methods are uniformly implemented throughout the entire curriculum. Materials and resources have been honed and refined over the nine years of the program's existence. Administration and faculty are enthused about the positive changes in their students and, overall, there were minimum problems in implementing and sustaining individualized instruction based on students' learning styles.

CHAPTER 5

Robeson High School—A Large Public School in Urban South Chicago

6835 South Normal Boulevard
Chicago, Ill. 60621
Contact Person: Jacqueline Simmons, Principal
(312)723-1700

T HE SOUTH SIDE OF CHICAGO RESEMBLES the panorama of many American cities. Beautiful old Victorian homes on wide, tree-lined streets mix with burned-out, windowless brick apartment houses that silently describe the socioeconomic and human relations problems of the people who live nearby.

It is in this conglomeration of edifices that Paul Robeson High School serves 2,300 students who represent each of the financial levels depicted by the area's architecture—wealth, middle and low income, and poverty.

The school's student population is equally representative of varied academic levels. Some excel and are admitted into fine, four-year colleges; others complete high school and immediately seek employment; and others struggle for marginal grades and eventually drop out.

When we first saw the adult "monitors" in Robeson's hallways, we thought that the school must have discipline problems. Quite the opposite; the youngsters consistently conducted themselves with decorum. Laughter was prevalent and camaraderie apparent, but the young people moved through corridors pleasantly, politely, and, if not totally quietly, in a mannerly fashion.

But, beyond the good behavior, students exuded a sense of well-being; they were positive, controlled, involved, and apparently glad to be there. Participation in scheduled classroom activities often seemed exuberant, but always reflected interest and a desire to learn. Students worked alone, in pairs, in small groups, and with their teachers as the activities or the instructor required. Choices were available so students could seek assistance from a classmate, the teacher, or an alternative resource.

In each class, a few students, apparently less comfortable in conventional seating, elected to sit on a carpeted section of the floor; others relaxed in the chairs that were available.

Again and again, Robeson students enthusiastically provided anecdotes to explain how they had repeatedly failed subjects until the school's learning styles program was initiated in September 1986. Apparently, being told that they had strengths had lifted their spirits.

Then, when they were shown how to study through their strengths and how to help themselves learn through their styles, many became sufficiently motivated to try. We frequently heard stories about how youngsters were achieving better than they had previously and how much they liked school now.

The students all seemed to know their learning styles and believed that their teachers were really trying to help them succeed. In that respect, Robeson High School demonstrated the most refreshing approach to education we had observed in any urban school. It is a unique educational effort and a tribute to the principal and teachers who worked so diligently to improve instructional opportunities for the young people.

Role of Administration

Paul Robeson High School, part of District 33 within the Chicago Public Schools, encompasses three campuses and has been under the dynamic leadership of principal Jacqueline H. Simmons since it opened in 1975.

The main campus is housed in Robeson High School, the science division is opposite the athletic field in the Parker School, and Robeson Outpost, which offers alternative programs, is nearby at Kennedy King College. Just as namesake Paul Robeson—scholar, lawyer, actor, singer—would have probably liked to be most remembered for his efforts toward world peace, so Simmons—educator, intellectual, leader, innovator—focuses her energy on increasing student achievement and enhancing the educational experiences of students by accommodating their individual learning style preferences through responsive classroom instruction.

Part of the impetus for Simmons' commitment to learning styles is related to the revised evaluation standards of the North Central Accreditation Association (NCAA). North Central emphasizes educational outcomes in cognitive areas (communication skills development, facility in computational skills, applied reasoning skills) and affective areas (independence in thought and action, productive use of time, growth through character education areas). Thus, the synthesized objective of Robeson High School is to respond to all ability levels by complementing individual students' learning style preferences.

Our interviews with students, parents, and teachers indicated that Simmons is perceived as a highly effective educational leader and manager. During the summer of 1986, 30 of the 99 faculty members attended an inservice workshop on learning style diagnosis and prescription.

Following that workshop, and based on strong faculty support, Simmons decided to phase in instructional changes beginning with the incoming 594 freshman students and their teachers. Subsequently, all ninth-grade students' learning styles were identified and they, their teachers, and parents were made aware of the results. The principal, freshman coordinator, and inservice education coordinator met regularly with the parents of the ninth graders to discuss educational goals and instructional approaches.

Initially, the teachers completed the *Teaching Style Inventory* (Dunn and Dunn, 1977), which assesses faculty members' instructional planning, teaching methods, student groupings, room design, teaching environment, evaluation techniques, educational philosophy, and characteristics.

Based on the discrepancies between the *Teaching Style Inventory* and the students' learning style data, teachers were encouraged to develop short-term goals for moving toward learning-styles-based instruction. Each teacher of ninth-grade students then developed between one and three short-term goals related to the environmental, physical, emotional, sociological, or psychological areas of learning styles; they also scheduled target dates for completion. Simmons filed these goal statements from each teacher on index cards and refers to them in her periodic conferences with individual faculty members.

Jewel Lewis, a science teacher, was appointed learning styles coordinator, and was released from all teaching responsibilities to work with teachers on inservice activities. Two other teachers, Barbara Vines and Margartha Smit, developed a range of materials and resources to accommodate varying student preferences for auditory, visual, tactual, or kinesthetic resources. They also use learning style homework disk-printout information for the ninth grade peer tutoring program.

Lewis reported that initially only science teachers sought her assistance when revising instructional strategies. However, after several months, colleagues in other disciplines also invited her into their classrooms to solicit suggestions for approaching difficult subject matter and concepts in ways responsive to a broad range of student differences.

She reported that "Teachers and students are more excited about learning than ever before. Our ninth grade teachers also instruct tenth and eleventh graders who are requesting transfers into those teachers' classes because of the learning styles approach. To them, it is more appealing than traditional instruction."

Teachers of sophomores began using learning styles-based instruction during the 1987-88 academic year, after a second summer workshop for 20 additional teachers was conducted. Therefore, with the opening of school in 1987, approximately half the faculty members were teaching to students' learning styles. They were supported and monitored by the inservice staff members and Simmons.

Observations

We heard many stories from students about how difficult school had been for them before learning styles, and how good they felt at Robeson. They easily accepted the concept that everyone learns differently but that everyone can learn.

They denigrated no one—not those who needed to use games or other tactual devices to study, not those who insisted they could think better when they ate, not those who said they preferred to sit by themselves and learn alone.

We had expected to find big city kids intolerant of instructional resources often believed to be appropriate for elementary youngsters, such as flip chutes, Pick-A-Holes, or task cards. Instead, most of the students with whom we spoke either accepted that those merely were alternative ways to learn or defended their usage vehemently because they enjoyed working with tactual materials.

In fact, one youngster who looked as if he could have been a Chicago Bears fullback, said that he had learned all the parts of speech *for the first time* by using an electroboard. Another reported that he had learned all the commands for the computer math program with the same device.

In almost every classroom, teachers worked with youngsters on difficult concepts by permitting them to focus on the same objective, but through preferred sociological patterns. Thus, some chose to work by themselves; others studied in pairs or in small teams. Those who elected to do so worked directly with the teacher.

The techniques observed most frequently at Robeson were Team Learning to *introduce* new material, and Circle of Knowledge to *reinforce* what had been taught previously. Students apparently were familiar with the strategies, for they formed their groups quickly, quietly, and conscientiously, and worked diligently and cooperatively.

After a designated interval, the teacher drew the material together by calling on individuals from each group. Students always illustrated their answers on the chalk board for global/visual learners, answered questions from classmates, and took pains to explain what was not understood. The peer tutoring that was evidenced was most impressive.

Classrooms reflected an active, participatory student body. Homework often required the development of original materials to demonstrate the students' expanding knowledge. Thus, the walls boasted the charts, three-dimensional panoramas, games, and tactual materials that students had made.

As in most other high schools, the youngsters told us that they had learned by creating the resources, but that classmates had profited by using those student-developed items as instructional resources—ways that they found easier to learn from than either a teacher's lecture or their textbook. Many obviously were proud to tell us that their peers had learned through their homework creations.

The rooms were alive with color. Encouraged to demonstrate their understanding of new knowledge in creative ways, students had put their talents to work. Mounted items were well done and attractive but, better than that, they described the objectives with which each class was involved. It was not possible to visit a ninth-grade room and not know what had been studied a week or two before.

In addition, many teachers capitalized on the students' strong tactual/kinesthetic preferences. They built in activities that required youngsters to dramatize, pantomime, demonstrate, explain without words, and move while learning.

For example, in a personal development class, the teacher wanted to emphasize the value of cooperation when working with others. She assigned students the task of building a tower from soda straws.

Youngsters were permitted to work as they chose—individually, in pairs, or in teams. As the towers rose, more and more youngsters began to interact seriously to solve the problems that developed. After a given amount of time, the youngsters were asked to describe the process of building the tower and any new things they had learned.

What emerged were insights into interpersonal relationships, scientific rules, building strategies, aids that could be used, and so forth. As an outgrowth, the many different perceptions were shared, and youngsters learned by doing rather than merely listening or observing.

Students' learning style printouts were available to them and were synthesized in charts and graphs throughout the school. Youngsters accepted their individual differences graciously and enjoyed telling about how they learned to learn through their strengths rather than their weaknesses.

In the mathematics and reading labs, students worked on individual objectives through their own learning styles. Therefore, some worked with a computer program, others used the same program but added a tape that read it to them. Some used a book; others worked with electroboards.

Barbara Vines, teacher and a staff developer, confided that she had been a traditional teacher. She'd had problems with groups of youngsters working away from her direct supervision and had been concerned about losing control of the class.

Once into learning styles, she forced herself to permit as many as six different groups to work on their own. She had also adopted a "P System"; if students did not achieve well on a test, she gave them a "Grade Pending" citation. Rather than let them fail, she permitted them to study more and retake the test.

Vines' description of the zeal with which students attack the information they had not conquered on the first exam, and how frequently they do well on that test the second time around, was corroborated by other teachers who had experimented with the same system.

Apparently, students are more motivated than they are given credit for, and when provided with alternative resources through which they can achieve, many will devote the time and effort necessary to do so. Unfortunately, some need either more time or a different process.

Vine reported that time, by itself, does not appear to be an answer. Because they require a great deal of structure and assignments divided into small, manageable subsets, many of her previously failing students need to learn what they can first; be tested to demonstrate what they already have mastered and what still remains; and then work on the facts or skills that eluded them during the initial round. Thus, when they learn the material gradually, they can deal with the unmastered requirements in steps or stages.

Robeson High School has introduced learning styles into its ninth grade curriculum in mathematics, reading, science, social studies, and reading across-the-board; other teachers are experimenting with pieces of learning styles in their subjects, too.

For example, Bertha Buchanan, the physical education teacher, uses role playing. When she found that no scripts existed that made sense to her street-smart, sophisticated, physically and emotionally mature students, she encouraged them to write their own. Many did. They wrote, memorized, and performed. They became so good at it that Buchanan invited other classes to see the skits. Students were so taken with the non-preaching, open, deal-with-it-directly presentations that they requested repeat performances and told neighborhood friends about the skits. Eventually, other schools invited the group to their buildings to perform, and a videotape was made of the entire series.

Of the more than 40 ninth graders whom we stopped, interviewed, and tape recorded, almost all were well aware of their styles and how to use their strongest characteristics to study and remember. Some knew how to bypass the teacher's style if it was "wrong" for them.

Robeson uses a homework disc developed by a Texas educator for her husband's marching band group.* (Texas has a "no pass, no play" rule, requiring that students who fail academics must refrain from participating in sports and all cocurricular activities.) The disc helped her husband's students pass their subjects and remain in the band. It has become widely adopted throughout the United States in schools working with learning styles instruction, and is being used effectively at Robeson.

Vines told us, "Our entire school system is moving up because the kids in our reading and math labs who used to fail are having their scores go up. More of them are doing homework than before!"

Margartha Smit, another Robeson inservice trainer, has pioneered the development of alternative materials through which students may learn identical objectives differently. She employs a Programmed Learning Sequence (PLS) that divides all written material into small sections; questions are posed about each subsection and answers are placed onto the back. Students gradually are led through all the information, but in small doses. PLSs have many visual and tactual activities interspersed among the readings.

Smit also uses a Contract Activity Package (CAP) system which outlines the unit by identifying clearly written objectives that must be mastered, but includes creative ways of demonstrating knowledge and sharing the activities that students develop.

Small-group techniques are built into the CAP to permit learners to work with peers if they find the material difficult. A CAP also includes a test

---

*The Homework Disc is available from the Learning Styles Network, St. John's University, Utopia Parkway, Jamaica, N.Y. 11439.

related to the objectives. Smit has developed several PLSs and CAP pairs for her students, but she also has made some for the teachers for whom she provides inservice. Thus, Robeson teachers are taught through *their* learning styles when provided inservice to learn how to work with their students' styles.

Smit recounts that before learning styles were introduced at Robeson, many of her students seemed to be overwhelmed by too much text, too few pictures, too many pages, or too many questions in their textbooks.

For visual youngsters who need structure but who are not motivated, she uses the PLS instead. She reported that now, "Nothing phases the youngsters. They have become confident. They now know they'll learn it."

Another nontraditional class that uses learning styles is Stuart Swift's *Law in American Society*. Swift has converted studies about government, society, and the law into a series of role playings in which students study the ramifications of specific problems and legal points, develop a script, and dramatize it to demonstrate their positions. Local attorneys visit, speak, and critique the scripts and/or acting. No one can remember when a student last cut this class.

The emphasis on conflict resolution and problem solving appears to be highly motivating to young people, particularly when the problems are ones they either face or read about on a daily basis.

Jewel Lewis, the science teacher who was released from teaching responsibilities to provide inservice for teachers in their classrooms, developed Multisensory Instructional Packages for both students and the teachers she trains.

In the beginning, she was sought solely by those who were willing to "try something different," but when their successes were noted by their colleagues, those teachers requested her services to learn more about learning styles. Lewis states that she sees teachers who are happier than they have ever been, often because what they are doing is not the same old thing, and because the new strategies are working.

By September 1987, half of Robeson's staff had received inservice training. The ninth graders who originally were introduced to the learning styles model became tenth graders and, thus, the program moved up to that grade. The new, incoming ninth graders were tested for their styles and the process began again.

Lewis' goal for herself is to design a CAP for teachers to help them demonstrate their commitment to students' learning. She believes that classes of approximately 20-28 students each deserve that commitment from their teachers.

Conclusions and Recommendations

Paul Robeson High School is a large, urban institution that is working to change its traditional approach to instruction. The school completed its first year of learning styles implementation by working predominantly with 30 teachers of freshman students. Plans are in place for repeating the process with the next class of ninth graders, expanding it into the sophomore classes to continue the work with the previous year's freshmen, and then gradually including upper levels in subsequent years.

The process of change has been well conceptualized. The principal serves as the instructional leader, consulting regularly with the learning styles coordinator and staff members, and involving parents in understanding and facilitating instructional goals.

Learning styles approaches are implemented across discipline areas and include the reading and mathematics laboratories and English, physical education, mathematics, science, social studies, special education, and vocational education classes.

There is a broad range of student academic ability and achievement levels. Selected students take college courses at nearby Kennedy King College, compete and win in the local science fairs for innovative problems and experiments, and enter prestigious colleges after graduation.

Chapter 1 students receive remediation in reading and mathematics, and are monitored carefully throughout their high school experience. Some of these students are among the top 10 graduates each year and, in 1987, 73 percent of those registered were graduated from Robeson High School.

The next steps for Robeson High School administrators and faculty members include the adoption of a more formal evaluation system for monitoring the effects of learning styles on student achievement, attitudes, and behaviors. In addition, the translation of difficult subject-matter units into alternative resources for learning identical information and skills will be continued.

Efforts by teachers to redesign textbook information so that it may be used effectively by independent and motivated, as well as dependent, unmotivated students will be continued, but students may also develop the materials. They will learn in the process and other youngsters will gain by having those resources available when necessary.

CHAPTER 6

Cedar Crest High School— A Large Public School in Rural Pennsylvania

105 E. Evergreen Rd.
Lebanon, Pa. 17042
Contact Person: Philip T. Kelley, Science Department
(717) 272-3178

A MONG THE ROLLING HILLS OF Pennsylvania Dutch country, Cedar Crest High School provides an inspiring example of what concerned, energetic faculty members can produce in only eight months of working with learning styles-based instruction.

And it is the faculty that provided the leadership for moving into this program; the administration underwrote the cost of some basic training and, at times, both encouraged and discouraged total involvement, but this was a teacher leadership effort almost from the beginning.

Cornwall-Lebanon School District has five schools (three elementary, one middle, one high school) with a total student population of 4,000. The parents and community members value education, as evidenced by a 2 percent dropout rate. The community is largely rural and small town, with 80 percent of its students bused to school. The facilities are functional and modern, lending themselves to environmental adaptation of the learning style approach within classrooms.

Although workshops on learning styles originally involved 133 teachers—approximately one half the district's staff—the high school is the major focus here.

Phil Kelley, in search of a dissertation topic, wanted to use different teaching methods with his high school science classes to determine the best way to help students master difficult topics. During a meeting with his superintendent, Edward Phillips, the learning styles research was discussed.

Subsequently, Kelley sought district support to attend a week-long training institute on the topic. In addition, the district contracted for a four-day, on-site workshop about how to teach in, administer, supervise, and evaluate a learning styles program for interested teachers and supervisors. Kelley was part of the workshop staff.

During those four days, Kelley and other high school teachers who had been using learning styles as a basis for their teaching in other districts and

31

other disciplines shared their experiences, enthusiasm, and how-to-start tips with the Cedar Crest High School faculty.

Teachers were encouraged to try a number of practical suggestions, but to choose only those that made sense to them personally. Nothing was mandated; teachers had the option of either ignoring or adopting as much as they wished of the learning style program.

Shortly after school began in September 1986, all 1,300 students at Cedar Crest High School were tested to identify their learning styles. Twenty of the almost 80 teachers on staff experimented with some strategies for responding to student characteristics. The students' profiles were discussed, explained, and shared with them and, when appropriate, were also shared with counselors, tutors, and parents.

Kelley assisted colleagues who wished either information or a helping hand; he also gave a second introductory workshop for those teachers who had not attended the August series but who were developing interest in what the others were doing.

With district approval and support, he planned a follow-up "advanced" workshop for summer 1987. In addition, he personally tried many of the style-responsive techniques he had learned about during that year.

Role of Administration

The principal, Joseph W. Hartman, attended the four-day learning styles workshop conducted in the school district in August 1986. The approach appealed to him in many ways: its responsiveness to individual differences, the management system that could be introduced gradually based on faculty interests and expertise, and the low cost of implementation.

He had reservations, too; he was concerned with how the conservative community would respond to students playing Walkman radios or nibbling on food while they were doing assignments. Yet, he wanted to encourage his staff; he was delighted with the interest and excitement many teachers displayed.

The district superintendent and the high school principal collaborated in a number of ways during the planning phase of the program. Initially, they exposed faculty members to the new educational concepts and strategies through inservice education and looked for a consensus among the faculty as to which approaches they assessed as valid before implementing change.

In addition, they arranged through a local university for teachers to receive graduate credit for attending summer workshops. Lastly, there were plans for a teacher incentive program for those who continue with inservice work and make adaptations within the classroom, but those have not materialized to date.

Observations

It was not possible to visit the classroom of every teacher who volunteered; however, the 15 classes that we did observe were impressive, as were the teachers' ability to use the techniques they demonstrated. Because they had a choice of which aspects to implement, many tried things that others had not and then elected to share successes and problems with colleagues.

In addition, several teachers had adapted previously used strategies to the newer understanding; thus, although they may have used peer teaching in the past, they currently use it only with those youngsters whose learning style profile indicated they liked learning with others.

We saw small-group strategies—Team Learning, Circles of Knowledge, and Brainstorming—used to introduce or reinforce hard-to-understand information. In some cases, students had been assigned to groups based on their learning styles; in other instances, they were permitted to choose with whom they learned.

We saw high school students learning from tactual and/or kinesthetic resources; in two classes, the youngsters were actually making these resources to facilitate learning and retention.

Susan Bensing, a communication skills teacher, encouraged the expression of feelings and perceptions by providing opportunities for students to demonstrate "through their tactual talents" those that were important to them. Thus, some painted, others molded, a few built, some sewed or crocheted. Each project was signed and mounted for all to share.

Shirley Jackson, an English teacher, asked the students to work in small groups. One or two students looked up answers; one or two developed the tactual materials such as Pick-A-Hole, electroboards, learning circles, or multisectioned task cards; a third or fourth youngster checked the completed materials against the test's answers.

For a unit on the Middle Ages, Jackson's students developed large wall hangings depicting the literary, political, economic, and cultural activities of that period.

We saw students working alone, in pairs, and in teams. No one ridiculed another's efforts; all seemed serious, sober, and intent on the task.

Tim Bixler, a science teacher, told us that he had expected his high school students to deprecate activities that required kinesthetic involvement, but that those who had made such choices seemed deeply involved and apparently enjoyed the assignment. Those who had selected more conventional ways of demonstrating their knowledge seemed interested in their classmates' finished products.

Again, we were told that students' grades had either improved or remained the same, but that discipline had improved immeasurably, as had student interest and motivation.

Phil Kelley experimented with translating textbooks into three alternative ways of learning the same material—Contract Activity Packages (CAPs), Programmed Learning Sequences (PLSs), and tactual/kinesthetic resources.

We saw eleventh grade science students working on these materials while seated wherever they felt physically comfortable.

Students occasionally spoke quietly with each other. Sometimes, a student stretched and took a moment of relaxation. The feeling of the class was industrious but not frenetic; cohesive but not large-group; individualized but not isolated.

Guidance counselor Ruth Maud said, "I've been working with students' study habits in relation to their learning styles. Just this morning we were planning next year's schedule for a resource room student. Afternoon is her best time of day, so she wanted to schedule vocational education in the morning and her academics in the afternoon, because those are harder for her."

Maud's efforts to counsel students through their learning style strengths have not been evaluated officially but she reported that students' feedback has been highly laudatory.

Conclusions and Recommendations

Cedar Crest High School represents a school in the first year of learning style implementation. It is characterized by administrative support for the program, a significant number of faculty members experimenting with a variety of different strategies to accommodate individual differences, and enthusiasm among students.

The superintendent recognizes the need to provide longitudinal learning experiences for students so there is continuity throughout the school years.

We observed many faculty members providing for sociological preferences and perceptual strengths. In most instances, however, differing preferences for structure, intake, design, and time of day were not accommodated, although a counselor is using time-of-day preferences in course scheduling to program students for their more challenging, difficult subjects.

We were favorably impressed by Kelley's leadership and by what he and his colleagues effected in a relatively short period of time. It is anticipated that, as student achievement and student behavior and attitudes improve, other teachers at Cedar Crest High School will begin to experiment with selected aspects of the program.

Toward that goal, we recommend the development of a comprehensive evaluation plan wherein changes that result as an outcome of learning styles instruction be identified in academic, attitudinal, attendance, behavioral, and self-concept areas.

CHAPTER 7

P. K. Yonge—A Small Laboratory School Affiliated with the University of Florida

1080 S.W. 11th St.
Gainesville, Fla. 32611
Contact Person: John M. Jenkins, Director
(904) 392-1554

T HE P. K. YONGE LABORATORY SCHOOL of the University of Florida, a K-12 demonstration model supported by the state legislature, accommodates approximately 900 youngsters and 58 faculty members. The school boasts a waiting list of 2,000 applicants, many of whom were registered for admission at birth.

The early childhood, elementary, middle, and secondary wings of the school are separated by park-like groves interspersed with benches, play and gymnastic equipment, and well-cared-for landscaping. The school climate reflects its environment—warm, sunny, gregarious, easygoing, interactive, and supportive.

Despite the many applications for admission to the school, registration reflects the population of the State of Florida. Legislative mandate requires that the student body represent, in exact percentages, the state's racial and socioeconomic groupings. The school's commitment to teaching each student individually is what led to its involvement with learning styles.

Role of Administration

The organizational structure of P. K. Yonge Laboratory School is unusual in that John Jenkins, the chief executive officer, serves as its director as well as a middle level administrator in the School of Education at the University of Florida. Because the school is funded by the state, the governing body of the school is the Board of Regents instead of a traditional school board.

There are two principals—one for K-8, and one for 9-12. In K-8, there are 60 pupils at each level (a total of 540) and approximately 38 teachers. In 9-12, there are 90 pupils in each grade (a total of 360) and 20 teachers.

Unlike many laboratory schools, P. K. Yonge has an identity apart from the University and enjoys a high degree of autonomy in determining its own policies and priorities. New students are usually selected for enrollment at the kindergarten level and at the beginning of high school. The student body is unusually stable, with minimal attrition.

The teachers at P. K. Yonge have master's degrees and more than one-half of the teachers in the secondary school are knowledgeable about learning styles and have implemented at least some aspects of this approach in their classrooms. The middle school principal, Jean Brown, supports learning styles-responsive instruction and is a doctoral candidate pursuing research in this area. She provides strong leadership for faculty members who are committed to implementing this approach. The high school principal, Chris Morris, is perceived by the faculty members as a highly effective administrator, but her leadership philosophy is to be responsive to teachers' interests rather than to mandate change.

Thus, P. K. Yonge's elementary and middle school divisions moved into learning styles approaches several years earlier than the high school.

When Wes Corbett, the psychology teacher, became interested in both the Dunn, Dunn, and Price Learning Style Inventory and the NASSP Learning Style Profile, he introduced the concept to the high school students he counseled in a teacher adviser capacity and was impressed with their interest in their own styles.

His original assignment was for the youngsters to compare the two instruments' assessments of their characteristics with their perceptions of themselves. They then were invited to describe the type of class that might be best for them, based on their learning styles as described by these diagnostic tools. Students responded so positively that Corbett discussed additional involvement with learning styles with Morris. At the same time, several faculty members approached Morris with requests for some initial training in instruction based on learning style identification.

Morris and Corbett attended a two-day seminar on learning styles, and as a result decided to sponsor a three-day workshop for faculty members. Eighteen high school teachers volunteered for participation and, at the end of the series, most indicated intentions of experimenting with selected aspects. In fact, Morris reported that faculty members had rarely expressed the amount of enthusiasm they exhibited for the learning styles approach.

Observations

Prominent among the secondary school faculty members who are deeply immersed in learning styles is Gayla Beauchamp, the science teacher. Beauchamp has an extraordinary chemistry background but, because she spent many years working in industry, her knowledge of methodology was not based on a pedagogical background.

When she first began teaching, she was disappointed with students' lack of interest in science and their inability to master specifics easily. Thus, when she was introduced to teaching through learning style strengths, she found the approach very appealing.

Beauchamp's first year in adapting curriculum to individuals' styles immersed the students in the translation of the course objectives to be mastered into specific materials that they created. She taught her students to do that and then encouraged them to share their developed resources with their peers. Thus, within the first two semesters, she had Contract Activity Packages (CAPs) for highly motivated achievers, Programmed Learning Sequences (PLSs) for those who required a great deal of structure and who either were visual *or* motivated and only tactual or tactual/kinesthetic learners in a wide variety of science topics. She later began designing Multisensory Instructional Packages (MIPs) for underachievers.

We saw Beauchamp's students studying identical objectives through varied and alternative resources. The materials appeared to be well-designed and executed, and youngsters seemed absorbed while working with them. We questioned many students about how they used the resources and were told that others had developed them as part of their own class assignments.

When asked how they had chosen to work with the specific materials they were using, the responses invariably indicated that the students had been tested for their learning styles, were advised of which resources would facilitate mastery, and had found, through experience, that it was easier to learn that way.

Some students described how much they liked learning science through their learning styles. Others expressed delight with how easily they learned with projects designed by their peers. Apparently the diversity and type of materials appealed to many, as did the comparatively informal environment in which their instruction occurred.

Many students applauded the choice in sequencing permitted to them: Beauchamp provided identical assignments, but allowed students to complete them in any sequence that made sense to them. Whether it was the choice afforded or the opportunity to control their studying to a degree, many students were motivated by the opportunity to determine which projects, objectives, or assignments to complete first, second, third, or last.

Chet Buchanan, studying with a Dictionary of Chemical Solutions PLS made by Joey Magnusson, literally beamed as he displayed the PLS. "This is more interesting than our book," he said, "and I learn everything faster this way!" When questioned about his grades, he reported that he not only enjoyed learning with a PLS, he also had better grades than he had before.

Similarly, Nancy Hooten, an eleventh grader, was absorbed in studying Chemistry #1 with student-designed materials on the definitions of liquids. Beauchamp reported that learning styles technology had given her a way to teach diversified topics to different kinds of students. She explained that, "good students learn easily but when they can put their hands on something concrete and learn in ways that permit them to enjoy the process, they work at it longer and enjoy it more. They also remember more for a longer period of time!" She insisted that she has had less frustration and fewer failures since working with learning styles.

When she first introduced students to developing their own Contract Activity Packages, Beauchamp wrote the objectives for each unit and then required the youngsters to design Activity and Reporting Alternatives. Eventually they created several small-group techniques and made the tactual supplements.

Beauchamp claimed that the students "learned more by making the materials than they did from a whole-class lecture!" We witnessed this when we observed youngsters studying the configuration of each element through an electronic game. The student who had made it coached the players who were using it to learn.

Beauchamp's enthusiasm was shared by many of her peers who had also experimented with CAPs and PLSs with their students. Some thought that the diversity of materials intrigued the youngsters; others credited knowledge of how to choose the best materials for individuals based on individual styles. Regardless of the reason, they were positive about students' academic gains and were pleased with the excitement that learning styles instruction had generated among their young charges.

Norma Spurlock, a middle school teacher, completely redesigned her classroom environment to respond to individual styles. Thus, in the same room, some students studied informally on lounge chairs or in carpeted areas while others sat at conventional desks.

The room was divided into well-lit and dimly illuminated sections. Some students used headsets to block out extraneous sounds when concentrating; others were permitted to listen to music on Walkman radios.

Students worked alone, in pairs, or in small groups. Youngsters experimented to see whether they learned better or less well with certain types of resources, and became acutely aware of their progress. Alternatives were suggested when academic achievement was not commensurate with indicated potential. In most cases, performance was better than anticipated and better than during previous semesters.

Spurlock recounted an experience with one boy who had chosen a CAP on *The One-Eyed Cat*. That particular unit offered many choices and, concomitantly, less structure than usual. The young man consistently requested more direction: How many objectives would earn him an A? Which activities were preferred by the teacher? Was one better than another? Which resources would give the most information?

After consistently directing the student to discover for himself the answer to particular questions, Spurlock examined his learning style printout, which indicated that he needed a great deal of structure. She immediately redesigned his CAP to prescribe specific directives rather than to permit the many options it originally provided.

This awareness of students' special instructional needs is representative of the faculty as a whole—elementary through high school. The widespread use of tactual resources indicates recognition of the need for a hands-on approach to academics; the variations in techniques further demonstrate faculty willingness to respond to their students' unique traits.

Most teachers use Team Learning to introduce new and difficult information, and Circles of Knowledge to reinforce what was taught through the Team Learning. These small-group strategies permit youngsters to learn cooperatively while simultaneously reducing pressure and allowing sociologically preferred groupings.

Sue Arnold, who teaches language arts and compensatory education, has one of the most beautiful rooms we have ever seen in a school building. Arranged into sections that focus on specific learning styles, it is colorful, interesting, attractive, stimulating, and responsive to the multiple styles.

Middle school students may work alone or in pairs, on carpeting, beneath tables, elevated in an enticing loft well above the activities that permeate the environment, or among peers in a variety of groupings.

Underachieving youngsters appear to thrive within the environment and work independently and industriously. Students walk past Arnold's room and linger to gaze, discuss, and indicate their interest (and envy) in what is going on.

Arnold also uses small-group instructional strategies, PLSs, and CAPs to teach identical objectives. She uses multisensory packages because of the tactual/kinesthetic strengths of many of her students.

Eve Singleton, who teaches ninth grade earth science, appeals to kinesthetic students by having them role play, dramatize, and engage in simulations. In one exercise, she had students write formulas for 20 different compounds. Some students studied alone, others in pairs, others in small teams, and some with her directly.

She then distributed cards with the compound formulas printed on them and was certain that each youngster received one formula and one compound description—neither of which matched the other. The students were directed to walk around the room in a pattern and, as Singleton called out either the ion or the chemistry formula, the two students who had the matching cards had to call out, "Ionic Bonding," find each other, and place their matching cards together.

They then gave the teacher the two cards that paired correctly. Thus, two elements that formed a compound when combined, were highlighted through movement, visual accents, and verbal/oral reiteration. Sometimes three students' parts were required to join to form the ionic bonding.

The resource room teacher, Patti Rosenlund, utilizes learning styles as the basis of all her teaching. Her room reflects consideration for multiple styles; her methodology incorporates every instructional strategy responsive to learning style differences and her discussions with students reveal their knowledge of their own styles and respect for each others' characteristics.

Rosenlund teaches through games, Multisensory Instructional Packages, Programmed Learning Sequences, small-group strategies, and tactual/

kinesthetic materials. Her records demonstrate the increased achievement that resulted from using learning styles-based instruction, and her students' attitudes and behavior indicate that they appreciate her efforts.

Space permits descriptions of only a representative sample of the middle and high school teachers involved in P. K. Yonge's learning style program. Others use even more dramatic techniques for reaching students through their learning styles.

Conclusions and Recommendations

P. K. Yonge Laboratory School is in the third year of learning styles implementation. Learning styles techniques are fully implemented by some faculty members, and partially implemented by others.

In general, teachers tend to implement those elements of the learning styles model that they deem important and critical to the instructional process. For example, some faculty members emphasize perceptual strengths and the development of multisensory materials based on auditory, visual, tactual, and kinesthetic modalities, while others accommodate the sociological preferences of students by providing individual, team, peer, teacher, or small-group activities.

The high school principal recognizes her role as instructional leader and is committed to becoming more and more knowledgeable about learning styles and their impact on achievement, attitudes, and discipline. Prior to our visit, she had only a minimum background in learning styles and was not in a position to exert direct leadership with the faculty. However, after attending a two-day institute on the topic, her own interest flourished and, gradually, she became both highly supportive and enthusiastic.

At one point, she expressed an interest in pursuing doctoral studies in this area because of her excitement about the potential of this kind of instruction.

There are plans to evaluate the impact of learning styles in selected classes. At present, the middle school principal and a teacher have tested seventh and eight graders to identify their sociological preferences for learning alone, in pairs, in teams, or with the teacher, and are planning to measure student achievement in science resulting from matched and mismatched treatments in individual versus small-group settings.

Generally, faculty members are very conscious of the need to evaluate the results of change, because the laboratory school concept attracts many visitors who are interested in educational innovation. Several faculty members have written textbooks and articles. In addition, there has been discussion of a cooperative publications project wherein the teachers will describe their experiences with learning styles in their classrooms and the administrators will describe theirs when planning the program.

CHAPTER **8**

Blake Middle School—A Small Private School in Minnesota

10 Blake Road
Hopkins, Minnesota 55343
Contact Person: Linda Cohen, Acting Director
(612) 938-1700

PULL OPEN THE HEAVY OUTER DOOR to the Blake Middle School library and enter a world reminiscent of medieval castles, pomp, and ceremony—a world populated with beautiful stained-glass windows, a ceiling-high organ, coats of arms depicting centuries of family descendants, and intricately woven tapestries and flags.

Were the knights of King Arthur's round table to appear, they would complement the old-world chapel perfectly, for it reflects life as it might have been within the castles of centuries gone by—with one exception; the hall is alive with the radiance of sunlight sparkling on the golden chains worn about the throats, wrists, or ankles of Blake's many students who find it a sanctuary for reading and doing their homework.

The corridors outside are another matter. They are alive with teenagers' laughter and vitality. Students walk from class to class with an unsupervised sense of purpose. Their mood is positive but light, their behavior is mature but casual. Students reflect the qualities that tend to be highlighted at this small, private school. Learning is important, but *how* each learns is an individual choice. Instructors teach to all styles, but it is the responsibility of every learner to apply what their teachers recommend.

The faculty at Blake is exceptional. Steeped in learning styles information, these creative, energetic teachers devote all their professional time to identifying their students' strengths and creating lessons that complement multiple styles. However, they also teach students how to teach themselves and to use the information provided by their learning style printouts to advantage.

Every room that we visited reflected the teacher's efforts to respond to multiple student styles. However, perhaps of greater importance, every teacher with whom we spoke emphasized belief in individual differences, knowledge of the extent to which instruction should be diversified, and a willingness to provide multiple resources and alternatives to assist their students in gaining mastery of the curriculum.

The faculty members at Blake personify what we believe to be the ideal—a knowledgeable, committed group of professionals exerting all their energies toward producing an excellent educational system for their highly achieving, often gifted students.

The Role of Administration

The Blake Schools are private, nonsectarian, suburban schools composed of three levels—one elementary school (K-5), one middle school (6-8), and one high school (9-12). The system is governed by Headmaster John Standard and a Board of Trustees charged with determining educational policies and practices. The majority of students pay an annual tuition of $5,000 and progress through the system for the full 13-year term.

In actual practice, each level within the system enjoys a great deal of autonomy, evidenced by the fact that the middle school has adopted a learning styles approach while the elementary and high schools adhere to traditional instruction.

Awareness of learning styles developed when the middle school director read *Student Learning Styles: Diagnosing and Prescribing Programs* (NASSP, 1979). Linda Cohen was so impressed with the contents that she subsequently joined the NASSP/St. John's University Learning Styles Network.

Convinced that an eclectic instructional program had merit, she embarked on faculty inservice programs using many of the Teacher Inservice Packages (TIPs) available through the Network.

One of her first steps was to solicit teachers at each grade level who represented a variety of discipline areas to form a Learning Styles Committee. Under Cohen's leadership, that committee arranged for:

- Assessment of all sixth graders' learning styles
- Parent-teacher-student conferences to discuss the youngsters' identified traits and the implications for home studying
- Funding from the Marbrook Foundation to provide for consultants and additional faculty workshops.

Recognizing that the change process is complex and that meaningful instructional improvement often begins with the teacher, the Learning Styles Committee encouraged the 32 middle school faculty members to identify their teaching styles and to understand the importance of expanding instructional strategies and techniques to accommodate more students' learning styles.

Faculty members have embraced the learning styles approach and have made significant changes in their teaching styles, emphasizing experiential learning to a greater extent than previously. The two areas that were immediately affected were responsiveness to sociological and perceptual preferences.

The majority of teachers provide for instruction through individual, peer, teacher-directed, and small and large-group patterns. They also use visual (graphs, diagrams, paradigms, films, illustrations, videotapes, chalk-boards), tactual (manipulatives, models, puzzles, computer software), auditory (lecture, discussion, instruction, audiotapes), and kinesthetic (experiential learning, role playing, simulations, experiments, body games and movement) approaches to teach new and difficult information.

The committee monitors the implementation of learning styles through questionnaires that ask teachers how they accommodate students' characteristics, and through discussions during biweekly Family Meetings, in which teachers discuss students for whom they are responsible. Those "families" are composed of faculty teams at each of the three grade levels.

In the next step of the implementation process, teachers moved from using whole-group strategies to accommodating diversified students' instructional needs through a variety of resources. A questionnaire distributed to faculty members one year after they had initiated the Blake Middle School Program revealed, for example, that sixth grade science teachers had been using auditory approaches to teach 50 percent of the time, whereas they had employed visuals only 15 percent of the time. Tactuals were used for only 5 percent of lessons; kinesthetic activities had been included for 30 percent.

When they discussed their findings and compared them with the information revealing that only 30 percent of students are auditory and 40 percent are visual (the remainder being either strongly tactual, tactual/kinesthetic, and/or possessing multiple strengths), the faculty members realized that they had been altering their teaching styles without direct knowledge of their students' individual perceptual strengths.

To further accommodate their students' styles, study units were developed to permit youngsters to choose the resources through which they would master their objectives. Thus, rather than teaching part of each lesson through lecture or discussion, part with visuals, part with a hands-on alternative, and part through an activity-oriented approach, teachers gradually began to indicate which objectives could be mastered through specific resources and then used different materials and methods for different students.

The approach required faculty members to develop class learning style profiles that summarized the strengths or preferences of students for each of many different variables. Thus, teachers used the students' diagnoses to recommend alternative ways of learning and to gradually develop varied ways of teaching identical subject matter.

Although some faculty members had concerns about managing the extent of diversity essential to responding to a broad range of learning styles, the mean class size at Blake Middle School and the high-achieving profile of the majority of its 265 pupils provide ideal conditions for this approach.

Observations

More than at any other school we visited, the teachers at Blake Middle School were highly responsive to students' perceptual preferences and consistently used several ways of teaching to objectives auditorially, visually, tactually, and kinesthetically.

The latter surprised us, for secondary school teachers often believe that when they "cover the curriculum" they have met their professional obligations. Instead, Blake's teachers demonstrated daily concern and caring for how well their students were learning and through which resources.

Kinesthetic teaching is by far the most difficult modality to include among a repertoire of strategies; few secondary teachers actually teach that way. At Blake, however, virtually all teachers relied heavily on activity-oriented strategies to demonstrate knowledge, and students responded with apparent enjoyment and demonstrated high achievement.

Richard Sabaka, a science teacher, responds to the mobility needs of his science students and provides avenues through which they can test their ability to conceive innovative creations that might help society. One of his assignments is to "make an invention that either is new or different, or creates another way of doing something that already has been done."

His students have to share their proposed ideas with him and describe the procedures that would be used; in that way, they secure a "patent" for their invention. Although the item could be designed and developed at home, it must be demonstrated in class.

The series of inventions that we saw were well-conceived, highly creative and, in many cases, ingenious. For example, one young man designed an alarm clock attached to a light switch. When the alarm goes off each winter morning, a battery is triggered and moves down to flip on his bedroom light. Thus, he need not get out of bed and stumble in the dark.

One student designed a device that waters plants while the homeowner is on vacation; another developed a Saran Wrap windshield wiper that automatically cleans the car window and removes insects while the driver is driving. A locker organizer was another invention. In one quick look, a student can locate tape, a mirror, a calendar and clock, a ruler, a calculator, pens and pencils, and any other items desired.

In his effort to present science through a variety of different methods, Sabaka has utilized all perceptual modalities. Perhaps because they have had so few opportunities to demonstrate their knowledge kinesthetically—by creating, role playing, dramatizing, or expressing scientific concepts through pantomime or dance—students often find the possibilities intriguing.

Sabaka reported that his plan to promote understanding of science and scientific concepts through varied modalities has increased student interest and helped youngsters with vastly different abilities succeed and enjoy science—sometimes for the first time. His students enter class enthusiastically and spend hours on their projects, discussing them at length and assisting each other with their development.

Teacher Steve Johnson found that the majority of his students had strong kinesthetic scores on their learning style printouts. Thus, when teaching social studies, he builds in dramatizations of as many aspects as possible.

During one fall semester, Johnson helped his classes identify those artifacts of their society that they believed people would find representative of their culture. Students learned how to safeguard those items for posterity and discussed how to bury them so that they would survive until discovered.

Johnson's spring classes learned how to discover buried artifacts, uncover them carefully, and analyze their impact on others. The youngsters simulated how to map a site and uncover artifacts by digging precisely, and how to notify the proper authorities. They then scouted the Blake grounds, found a buried treasure, uncovered items without harming them, and determined those artifacts' place in another society.

These eighth graders enjoyed social studies, took their assignments seriously, and developed a strong interest in learning about other cultures through archaeological methods.

Mary Ellen Kasak-Saxler makes the French language and culture come alive for her students. She uses multiple activities in each class period and involves her students in role playing, simulations, Team Learning, Circle of Knowledge, and kinesthetic activities throughout the day.

She encourages a high level of creativity among her charges, requiring that they either draw, pantomime, sing, dramatize, or demonstrate that they have learned what has been required.

She designed many exciting strategies to reinforce vocabulary by illustrating words and then building them into creative sentences with interesting props. For example, she used a furnished doll house to help the students verbalize the many items found in a home; they then expanded the words into phrases and sentences. Some students found responding to oral questions difficult, so Kasak-Saxler dramatized the meaning and asked students to respond in whichever modality they preferred.

Kasak-Saxler translates her curriculum into alternative methods for different students based on their learning styles. She also experiments with helping students use their strengths rather than their weaknesses to do their homework.

Bruce Jones' methods of teaching science to students through their learning styles provide a source of continuing excitement and involvement for the youngsters with whom he works. To demonstrate the need to use things other than human strength to move heavy objects, Jones loaded books into several heavy cartons. He then assigned students to teams and encouraged them to experiment with a variety of ways of moving the heavily weighted boxes from one section of the room to another and to lift them. He provided assorted props—such as sheets, planks, ties, straps, and slides—and encouraged the teams to accurately record the successes and problems they encountered with each.

Conclusions and Recommendations

Blake Middle School provides a unique approach to implementing learning styles-based instruction in that the initial impetus for change originated with the assistant director and faculty committee; the entire school then embraced this eclectic approach.

A combination of factors coalesced to ensure the success of the program, including strong leadership, grant monies to provide inservice workshops, parent involvement in understanding and supporting the concept by providing compatible learning styles home environments, and an ongoing commitment to evaluation.

Middle school youth are at an age that is characterized by rapid growth, physiological changes, and an unusually high energy level. Learning interventions must parallel student needs for mobility and activity. Hence, experiential learning or "learning by doing and experimenting" is essential.

Blake students were consistently engaged in archaeological digs, science projects, English activities, and social studies committee tasks that met their special needs.

Teachers have implemented specific aspects of learning styles very well, including provisions for students' sociological preferences and perceptual strengths. However, there has been little response to environmental, emotional, and selected physical needs such as intake and time-of-day. Since the program is in its second year of development, it is anticipated that additional approaches to learning styles will be adopted gradually.

The Learning Styles Committee, chaired by Linda Cohen, had a major role in planning, implementing, and evaluating the program. The committee members meet regularly to monitor its effectiveness and to poll faculty members about the extent to which they are accommodating students' styles.

To stimulate awareness, they constructed a large Learning Styles Tree and mounted it in the faculty lounge so that all teachers could see the "roots" and "germination" of the program.

CHAPTER 9

CLIP: An Alternative Program in Four Large Suburban Washington Schools

19400 56th Ave. West
Lynwood, Wash. 98036
Contact Person: Karol Gadwa, Director Clip Programs, and Principal
Scriber Lake High School
(206) 670-7270

THE DROPOUT PATTERN HAS BECOME SO severe that every professional organization in the nation is advocating concerted efforts to alleviate the problem and to reach the at-risk students.

The problem often begins with uneasiness during classes. Students stop paying attention, talk, daydream, or engage in nonacademic tasks. Before long they start coming late. As time goes by, the lateness becomes absence, accompanied by underachievement and antagonism.

One sensitive administrator foresaw the gravity of this pattern many years ago and assigned a young teacher, Karol Gadwa, to examine its causes and the possible steps that could be taken to prevent adolescents from beginning the destructive and sometimes suicidal trip from school to the streets.

This is the story of the emergence of learning styles in the Edmonds School District in Washington State. It demonstrates that dropouts can be brought back from alienation and despair.

Role of Administration

Edmonds School District No. 5, approximately 25 miles from Seattle, and the sixth largest district in the state, experienced a 32 percent increase in its dropout rate between June 1977 and October 1981. The superintendent assigned a team of educators to examine the dropout population, identify methods that would prevent more students from leaving school prematurely, and design programs to bring back and maintain dropouts until they were graduated (Gadwa et al., 1983).

Between September 1981 and February 1983, dropouts and their parents were interviewed and the youngsters' records were examined for teachers' comments concerning academic, health, and behavioral characteristics. All secondary students were administered the *Learning Style Inventory* (LSI) and their scores were compared to those of the tenth, eleventh, and twelfth grade in-school populations to determine whether significant differences existed between the two to provide a "typical dropout" profile (Gadwa et al., 1983).

The data indicated that students who leave school before graduation often show difficulty as early as kindergarten or first grade; however, during the beginning years of school, teachers usually provide sufficient support to compensate for educational difficulties. The dropouts in Edmonds reported that their academic difficulties peaked at the junior high level and led to failure, continual low achievement, boredom, feelings of rejection, frustration, and absenteeism. What soon followed was total withdrawal from school.

The learning styles of the dropouts indicated that, contrary to popular expectation, they were motivated to learn. They also were:

- Highly peer and teacher motivated
- Tactual and kinesthetic, and *not* auditory/visual learners
- Unable to sit for long periods of time
- In need of variety and alternative opportunities to learn alone, with peers, and with their teachers; they were unresponsive to consistent instructional routines and repetition
- Quickly bored when required to learn through patterns; thus, they remained on-task longer when permitted to structure how they did assignments
- *Not* early morning learners (Gadwa et. al., 1983).

These data were supported through interviews with the students and by appraisals of their teachers' written comments in anedoctal records. In addition, students' reactions to the LSI indicated that the data accurately described them and how they learned. Those identical characteristics were revealed in two other studies of dropout populations—Johnson (1984) in Maryland and Thrasher (1985) in Florida. These also paralleled Tappenden's (1983) findings for 2,000 secondary vocational education students in Ohio.

As a result of the district's study of its dropout population, a new program—Contracted Learning for Individual Pacing (CLIP)—was designed for adolescents whose styles were not being responded to in conventional classes. Gadwa was invited to direct this alternative program, which was initiated in February 1984 at Edmonds Community College. Programs were subsequently added at Edmonds High School, Mountlake Terrace High School, and Lynnwood High School. Gadwa was then named principal of Scriber Lake, a fifth district high school.

CLIP applicants range from 14 to 20 years of age and are referred to the program for a variety of reasons, including-poor attendance, under-achievement, and/or an inability to fit into traditional classes.

It is important to remember that dropouts from conventional schools often cannot tolerate having extensive external structure imposed on them. They learn much more effectively alone or with several peers than they do in large-group, teacher-controlled situations.

They rarely are morning people; instead they find it difficult to focus on demanding academic tasks when most schools begin, to say nothing of *getting to school on time!* They usually perform significantly better in an informal environment with soft music and natural lighting than they do under the glare of flourescent light rays hitting shiny desk tops.

Another reason many CLIP students feel restricted by traditional classes is that many are actively involved in out-of-school activities to which they are extremely devoted and which they believe may be their life's work. For example, 1986-87 CLIP students included several professional models, skiers, and skaters; others held responsible positions with industry and business. Some of these young people are mature adults who find much more excitement and positive challenge in employment than they do in school. They *do* want to complete their education, but they are sufficiently nonconforming and independent to believe they can do so through independent, self-paced studies.

CLIP features self-paced study in academic core disciplines. Thus, entering registrants are tested to identify their learning styles and then are guided into English, social studies, mathematics, health, and/or psychology (grades 9-12) through book units on a contract basis, computer-assisted instruction when available and appropriate, or experiential learning that is responsive to adolescents' strong kinesthetic and mobility needs.

To remain in CLIP, students must attend classes at least three and one-half hours daily and complete at least three units, or their equivalent of .50 credits, in each of six different courses each semester.

Former at-risk or turned-off students seem to thrive in CLIP's collegially-oriented environment where many choices of *how* and *when* they learn are permitted. However, a great deal of supportive structure is provided in terms of teachers who work closely with parents. If a youngster fails to attend class, the parent is phoned that same day.

Parent conferences are scheduled regularly, and focus on such themes as learning style differences between the student and parents (an inventory initially is administered to assess parents' learning styles), adolescent developmental concerns, self-esteem, facilitating positive behavioral and attitudinal changes, and career development.

Parent evaluations are obtained each semester. They rate their childrens' academic performance, attendance, and attitudes toward school both before and after entering CLIP. Parents generally perceive marked improvement in all areas and appreciate their involvement with CLIP personnel.

Program evaluation consists primarily of comparing student credits earned and attendance records prior to and after entering the program. A sample of CLIP I students' academic progress as reflected in credits earned appears in the box. Attendance records are equally impressive.

| | CREDITS EARNED: CLIP 1 STUDENTS | | |
Year	No. of Students	Semester Prior to CLIP	First CLIP Semester
1985	34	58	73½
1986	20	21½	58½

No soft-grant monies were received to sponsor this alternative program. Thus, the district must be commended for its concern for at-risk students. The foresight to research the causes of dropping out and to assign staff members to determine how to counter the movement must be credited to the Edmonds School District Central Office. But the cornerstone of the CLIP support system is its designer Karol Gadwa, a young, enthusiastic pioneer in the alternative education movement and a person whose creative energies soar when they are directed toward helping adolescents in or near trouble.

Observations

Visits to three CLIP sites provided different perspectives of the program based on facilities, the length of the teachers' experience in this alternative, and the type and amount of instructional resources available. The students, however, tended to be essentially similar in that they appeared to be more mature than most high schoolers. They were generally very outgoing, people-oriented, and community conscious.

During our visits to secondary institutions in the United States, we rarely met youngsters who were not willing to share their perceptions, but most revealed mildly negative attitudes toward comprehensive high schools. Those students faulted teachers for inflexibility, monotonous teaching, authoritarianism, and a boring curriculum; they seemed to believe that these characteristics were synonymous with schooling. Many told us that it was only after their teachers had begun to use learning styles that they learned.

CLIP students expressed much more antagonism to traditional teaching than we had heard previously. These students seemed emotionally hurt. Still, they were recuperating, often with the help of the closely knit contacts they had made with other CLIP students and their program teachers.

Students' descriptions of how their problems started were straightforward; they assumed the responsibility and guilt for their actions. These youngsters insisted that they had tried to negotiate the traditional system but that it had been so unresponsive to them that they believed the teachers, the school, and/or their parents did not care about them. Many students repeatedly stated that they had little respect for their previous schools' regulations, which were often perceived as arbitrary, capricious, and worthless.

CLIP students believe they can learn well if they are taught in ways they can understand; they do not believe that doing what they are told to do merely because the rules require it is worthwhile.

Attendance in the program is excellent, with only 2 of CLIP's 75 full-time and between 20 and 30 part-time students demonstrating erratic patterns. Students support each other and become achievement-oriented provided they are permitted options in procedures, techniques, and environments. Our interviews with CLIP participants revealed that they had strong educational and vocational focuses and well-developed plans for mastering graduation requirements and then moving into career choices. Typically, these young people are employed part-time in local restaurants and other businesses, and frequently find positions for their classmates. Several have very demanding managerial responsibilities.

Conclusions and Recommendations

The CLIP program in the Edmonds School District was founded on the principle that students learn in many ways and that individual differences must be addressed within the instructional environment. The teachers were carefully selected, are student-centered, and respond to individual learning styles on a daily basis. Curriculum mastery is emphasized and participants are responsible for acquiring the same skills, knowledge, and competencies as students in Edmonds' traditional high schools.

However, because so many of CLIP's students work together by choice, it would seem appropriate to introduce well-structured, small-group instructional strategies to help them learn. In addition, because CLIP's other participants enjoy working independently, the self-paced aspect of the program would be enhanced by a Contract Activity Package-type of instruction.

Finally, many of CLIP's students require a great deal of structure but are not independent learners; a programmed learning system would facilitate those youngsters' achievement. Several of the high schools included in this book encourage their students to develop these types of instructional resources.

The youngsters in CLIP certainly could translate required texts into instructional materials. With this single addition—the availability of resources which actually teach to diversified styles—CLIP would become an ideal alternative for the students for whom conventional instruction is ineffective.

CHAPTER 10

Franklin Township Middle School—A Large Suburban Indiana Public School

6019 South Franklin Rd.
Indianapolis, Ind. 46259
Contact Person: Sheri Patterson, Dean of Students
                                (317) 862-2446

I N THE 1980s, AT THE BEGINNING OF THE period of area growth, court-mandated busing was initiated in Franklin Township. Each day, minority children are brought from Indianapolis to this rural-turning-suburban school district.

Franklin Township Middle School is a long, modern, clean facility built during the mid-1970s. It houses a small, sober, dedicated core of teachers involved with teaching students in grades 6-8 through learning styles.

Role of Administration

Franklin Township's school system became involved with learning styles as a result of the conviction of four faculty members—Linda Dunn and Sharon Easley of Arlington Elementary School, and Jane Kitley and Sheri Patterson of Franklin Township Middle School.

In 1983, they attended a seven-day Leadership Institute on Learning Styles in New York City. Costs for their participation were paid by the school district with the understanding that they would return to Indiana one month later and conduct a three-day introductory workshop for their colleagues.

Excited and anxious about the 50 teachers who had registered for their workshop, the four transformed a typical high school classroom into a model learning styles design that included formal and informal areas where participants could work in small groups or alone; resources that taught the teachers how to teach their students through learning style; and fruit, sunflower seeds, popcorn, nuts, and lemonade.

The participants were so taken with the workshop room and the pleasure of learning through *their* styles, that many voted it the best workshop they ever had attended. Word spread, and the four were invited to conduct sessions in school districts throughout Indiana.

The four original proponents continued spreading the word through visits to other schools, publication of a newsletter, publicity generated by local newspapers, and direct involvement with administrators in the district. The following July, they returned to New York for advanced training but, this time, brought with them an elementary principal, Mike Wolpe, and the middle school principal, Lee Thompson.

In July 1985, Kitley and Patterson returned to the New York Institute for the third time, bringing Luanne Reabe, the resource room teacher from Franklin Central High School, with them. They described her as having done wonders with high school failing students by teaching them through their style strengths, rather than through their weaknesses.

Reabe was invited to write an article for the *Learning Styles Network's Newsletter* cosponsored by the National Association of Secondary School Principals and St. John's University (Reabe, Winter 1985).

One year later, in a second manuscript, Reabe described how Franklin Central had requested that she design a program to help underachievers succeed in their academic subjects. Progress Under Learning Styles (PLUS) targeted youngsters who had failed two or more subjects during the previous semester and guided them toward identifying their learning styles and then using their strengths to study, do homework, and take tests.

Provided as an alternative to study hall, PLUS was initiated during the last nine-week grading period of spring 1984. When students' grades had improved in 60 percent of their classes within that short period, the program was reinstituted for the 1984-85 year. Reabe reported that during the first nine-week period of the second year, 66 percent of the previously failing students achieved higher grades than during their entire high school experience. She also found that youngsters' self-esteem and confidence improved noticeably.

By the close of the 1985-86 year, the PLUS program had reaped even more substantial gains, not only in student achievement, but in how the participants felt about themselves and parental support. Reabe met with countless positive, grateful parents and excited, proud students who suddenly had developed a new perspective on schooling, their potential, and themselves (Reabe, Summer 1986).

In the meantime, Jane Kitley continued perfecting learning styles strategies at the middle school. She invited colleagues to work with her, provided several workshops, and, served as learning styles consultant in several states. In 1987-88, Kitley became the learning styles supervisor in Franklin Township.

Patterson, on the other hand, incorporated the instructional strategies into guidance and counseling in her role as dean of students at the middle school (Patterson, Autumn 1986). She encouraged administrators to provide continuing workshops on the subject as a support system for colleagues interested in syles-based instruction.

Lee Thompson, the middle school principal, and Mike Wolpe, the elementary school principal, also provided continuing support for and encouragement to their staffs.

Observations

Franklin Township Middle School

Jane Kitley is the middle school reading teacher. Her classroom has no wall-to-wall carpeting to permit relaxation in an informal setting—an environment preferred and needed by poor readers. Any dividers that permit subdivision of the larger space into dens, alcoves, or other sections in which youngsters might pursue their individual or paired assignments were created by Kitley; the school contributed little in the way of accessories.

Despite these problems, Kitley created a learning style classroom in which previously difficult-to-teach youngsters can function independently and succeed among their peers.

For example, she begins each lesson by providing her students with clearly-stated objectives so they become immediately aware of what they should master during that period. Students are provided auditory, visual, tactual, and/or kinesthetic resources through which they can learn what the objectives require. They are permitted to work in preferred sociological patterns: alone, in pairs, in a small group of three or four, or directly with Kitley.

The environment has been redesigned so that one couch is near the front of the room adjacent to a window in a well-lit area; another couch and two lounge chairs have been placed in the rear of the room in a somewhat less-illuminated section. Across the room, on an inside wall, are a few small rugs and pillows providing a more casual study area. Desks and chairs may be moved quietly to any part of the classroom.

Kitley teaches her students to work quietly; their voices are neither loud nor disruptive.

A typical lesson includes whole-class discussion of the objectives that have been printed either on the chalkboard or on a paper distributed to the youngsters. The students then consider how the objectives might be met and the resources available for doing so. Then students are reminded of their learning styles and the need for working the way they learn best—as long as they do not infringe on anyone else's style.

Youngsters are permitted to decide with whom and where in the environment they wish to concentrate and, gradually, they are released to pursue their studies. If individuals wish to speak with Kitley, there is a system for attracting her attention and waiting until she is free.

Her assignments encourage the use of small-group strategies for cooperative peer interactions; opportunities frequently are provided for independent projects and assignments based on identified individual needs.

Students quickly shift from individual or paired tasks to Team Learning or Circle of Knowledge. They seem to be cognizant of several such strategies used as part of weekly, if not daily classroom routines.

Discipline is excellent; although, according to Kitley and the school principal, she usually is assigned undisciplined students with many personal and academic problems. While interviewing Kitley's students, we were impressed with the sobriety with which they considered our questions. It was not unusual for them to recount stories of years of academic failure as well as their current successes. Apparently, what they had been taught in this class also carried over to their other subjects.

Students complete their assignments even while Kitley answers others' questions. They seek each other's help and have learned to use alternative resources such as tapes, programmed sequences, and tape recorded books. They also enjoy puzzles and word games, and Kitley has secured many of those to provide a source of fun reinforcement for previously taught concepts or skills.

Kitley also uses a system of optional bonus tasks that permit students to gain extra points toward their final unit grade. She suggests that the bonus assignments provide: reinforcement through varied perceptual strengths— particularly for tactual/kinesthetic students who are good with their hands and like projects; a way to keep underachievers involved academically after they have completed required work and thus avoid classroom management problems; an opportunity for underachievers to improve their performance and grades; and motivation for those who find learning difficult or unrewarding.

Jane Kitley and Sheri Patterson have shared their enthusiasm for teaching through student's learning styles with colleagues throughout Franklin Township. As a result, several other middle school faculty members use various strategies based on individual, rather than large-group approaches. For example, Linda Lamberth uses a game, *Typewriter,* to respond to the varied perceptual strengths of students.

For spelling, she divides her class into three teams. Each student in each team is given two letters, one on each of two different, large, white squares. Lamberth calls out a word from the class spelling list and the members of the team whose turn it is and who have those letters, must rise, move from their seats to the front of the room, position themselves into the correct letter sequence for that word, and call out the letters to spell the word correctly— all in a predetermined amount of time. Successful completion earns the team five points.

When the word is incorrectly spelled or the amount of time is exceeded, the next team has a chance to spell the word correctly within the allotted time.

Through this procedure, visual students *see* the word correctly spelled, auditory ones *hear it,* and most participate *kinesthetically.* Students who do not want to stand may choose to sit near the front and merely rise or reach to place their letters into the correct word sequence.

Sixth grade teacher Deb Beals also capitalizes on the research concerning perceptual strengths. Whenever working with underachievers who tend to be strongly tactual or tactual/kinesthetic, she encourages them to trace angles, shapes, numbers, or signs with their fingers.

She instructs the youngsters to close their eyes as they trace to eliminate visual distractors and help them concentrate tactually. Beals uses games for such students to further accent tactual learning, and often employs small-group strategies such as Circle of Knowledge to reinforce math skills.

In addition, she builds onto students' experiences to help them learn. For example, when teaching about obtuse angles, she tells students that an obtuse angle is more than 90 degrees and shows how wide it is when compared with right or acute angles. She then dramatically describes obese as being fat and suggests that obese and obtuse sound similar. She shows that a right angle is "right"—neither too fat nor too skinny, and then counters with, "If a right angle is just right, and an obtuse angle is fat, the remaining acute angle has to be the thin one—*less* than 90 degrees." The references to comparisons in their daily lives help students learn and remember.

Beals reported that her underachievers learned much more quickly and remembered longer when she related their math information to real-life situations. They performed even better when she permitted them to adapt their environment to how they believed they learned best. That arrangement also works well in study hall, where she permits students to sit at desks or on the floor.

Aware that global students often learn in the reverse way from analytic students, Carolyn Riley reverses specific techniques to provide youngsters with alternatives. For example, instead of posing questions for brainstorming and requiring small groups of students to develop answers, she occasionally posts the answers and directs groups of three to five students to think through what must have been the questions or problems.

She has experimented with Circle of Knowledge in the same way, reversing the strategy for different occasions. Riley's students are shown how to make tactual materials such as electroboards, multipart task cards, or learning circles to teach themselves difficult information. She has experimented with colored cellophane over sections of class lighting to provide a softened illumination.

Riley and a number of her colleagues repeatedly report that many students behave better, are more calm, have longer attention spans, and learn more than ever before when permitted to concentrate in ways that their learning style analyses suggest is correct for them.

Franklin Central High School

It would not be appropriate to describe the developing learning styles program in Franklin Township without detailing Luanne Reabe's work.

Reabe sensed that failing students were not stupid and that they could learn, but for some unexplained reason they always had difficulty.

She began working with learning styles by experimenting with tactual resources—task cards, learning circles, or electroboards—and found that not only did her students pay better attention and learn well from them, but that they could make their own materials and through them, teach themselves difficult information fairly easily.

She then used Multisensory Instructional Packages, Programmed Learning Sequences, and, for some, Contract Activity Packages. She was amazed to find increased achievement and improved attitudes within a few weeks.

Later, she noticed increased self-confidence among those who were using these materials. In addition, she began to hear students' comments describing their own realization that they were not "retarded," but merely needed to learn differently.

As described earlier, Reabe designed and implemented the high school's PLUS program and, within the first nine-week period, witnessed amazing gains. Such gains continued throughout the semester and into the next year.

Reabe devotes almost all her time either to developing materials for those youngsters who just cannot "make it" with conventional instruction or to teaching students how to teach themselves.

A few teachers at Franklin Township Central High School are working together to gradually adopt learning styles. Most suggested that when students who have failed are helped by learning styles methods, other teachers suspect that standards are being lowered. They agreed that it is important to translate research into easily digestible pieces so that teachers everywhere understand that individuals do vary significantly in how they achieve and that all styles should be valued, as long as the students do learn.

Conclusions and Recommendations

Franklin Township represents the only district-wide effort to implement learning styles-based instruction that we visited, and none attempted so much with so few trained persons. Teachers became involved in learning styles through their friendship with the two secondary trainers or their interest in the concept. Attendance at workshops was voluntary; implementation was strictly because of personal excitement.

Franklin Township has a small group of well-trained faculty members who could exert enthusiastic guidance for other teachers. However, it is our belief that the building administrators should provide more positive leadership than has previously been demonstrated. The middle school and high school principals need not demonstrate specific techniques; they *do* need to require participation, provide encouragement through their own attendance, follow up with supervision and discussions, and distribute articles describing the research on learning styles and its practical applications.

CHAPTER 11

Analysis of Change and Leadership Style

DURING THE PAST DECADE, EDUCATORS HAVE been exhorted to consider and provide for student individuality in learning rate and style. Goodlad (1984) suggested that provisions for learning style differences are not made in most schools:

> Our data suggest that . . . students worked independently at all levels but primarily on identical tasks, rather than on a variety of activities designed to accommodate differences. In general, there were more different kinds of instructional activities in elementary than in secondary classrooms; elementary school teachers varied the group configurations in their classrooms from time to time and occasionally even changed the content of their methods of teaching. Secondary teachers rarely individualized classroom procedures. On the whole, teachers at all levels apparently did not know how to vary their instructional procedures, did not want to, or had some kind of difficulty doing so" (pp. 105-106).

When summarizing the observations of hundreds of secondary school classrooms, he depicted the following scenario:

> The teacher sat at a desk watching the class, lecturing, or reading. Most students were writing, a few were stretching, and the remainder were looking contemplatively or blankly into space. The classrooms we observed were more like than unlike those in the old images so many of us share. Usually we saw desks or tables arranged in rows, oriented toward the teacher at the front of the room (p. 94).

> Four elements of classroom life in the schools of our sample come through loud and clear from our data. First, the vehicle for teaching and learning is the total group. Second, the teacher is the strategic, pivotal figure in the group. Third, the norms governing the group derive primarily from what is required to maintain the teacher's strategic role. Fourth, the emotional tone is neither harsh and punitive nor warm and joyful; it might be described most accurately as flat (p. 108).

The classrooms described above differed markedly from the ones we visited that utilized a learning styles instructional approach. Those we observed can be characterized as follows:

- The vehicle for teaching and learning is the individual student. Patterns within the classroom reflected pairs, small groups, or individuals working alone or with a teacher or aide. Those patterns changed with specific tasks or youngsters' preferences.
- The student is the pivotal focus; all learning is compatible with the student's assessed learning style preferences.

- The room design is innovative, with formal areas (desks, chairs, tables) and informal sections (carpeted with area dividers, pillows, soft chairs, and/or couches). Both bright and soft illumination often was available, and student clothing reflected individual needs for warm or cool temperatures.
- The norm is that each student assumes a major responsibility for learning and seeking environmental, physical, sociological, and psychological stimuli conducive to his or her requirements.
- The emotional tone of the group is exciting and supportive due to extensive student involvement in the learning process.
- Students are acquiring the required knowledge, skills, and competencies through a wide variety of strategies—tactually (drawing, charting, illustrating, notetaking), kinesthetically (role playing, demonstrating, experimenting), visually (filmstrips, computer software, reading), and auditorially (lectures, discussions, teachers' explanations, audiotapes, and peer-tutoring).

The literature suggests that moving from traditional instruction to learning styles-based instruction involves fundamental change, as described in the next section.

Planned Change

Planned change in schools is limited in scope, is directed toward enhancing the quality of life or the learning process among students, includes a role for students, and is guided by a professional practitioner who acts as a change agent (Kettner, Daley, and Nichols, 1985).

Sequentially, the change agent considers the possibility of improving the situation, develops a plan to guide the proposed change, and sees that the change is implemented. Usually, the change agent, although a central person in the process, works collaboratively with others.

Stages in the change process have been identified by a number of researchers (Bentzen, 1974; Bok, 1986; Goodlad, 1984). These stages are:

1. *Awareness:* developing initial recognition of change or innovation.

Awareness begins with a recognition that there may be a more effective system or approach to achieving the objectives established by the school or system. Awareness encompasses an acknowledged discontent with the existing system and the recognition that fundamental problems are not being addressed adequately. Such problems may include, but are not limited to, low student achievement, high rate of student failure, discipline problems, negative student attitudes, student apathy regarding learning, or a high rate of student absenteeism or dropping out.

In our interviews with change agents in the schools we visited, initial awareness usually was developed by one initiator with a core of other key persons within the system or school who generally met either formally or informally to discuss school-related problems, innovations, or practices.

Initial exposure to the innovation often resulted from the change agent's attendance at a conference, seminar, or convention, or interactions with persons in other school districts or state departments of education.

2. *Knowledge:* acquiring content and understanding of the change or innovation.

Acquisition of knowledge and understanding of the new concepts or procedures builds on the exposure gained during the initial stage, but involves a concerted effort for in-depth study of the change. The vehicle for acquiring knowledge about learning styles most frequently was the national conventions of either the National Association of Secondary School Principals (NASSP) or the Association for Supervision and Curriculum Development (ASCD).

The change agents had also become well-versed in learning styles approaches through regional or state seminars and workshops, professional journals and books, demonstrations, or consultants.

Because this stage is demanding, ongoing, and intensive, it frequently began with an attempt to educate the entire faculty about learning styles and the research supporting this concept. Ultimately, a core of respected teachers became knowledgeable while others rejected the change.

Despite that comparatively successful pattern, in the two private schools in which learning style concepts and practices had been embraced by the entire faculty, the administrator possessed both conviction regarding the merits of the change and the authority to mandate compliance. In one, participation was required; in the other it was voluntary.

3. *Personalization:* reflecting and internalizing the implications of the change or innovation.

Ownership is a critical concept in the change process, and teachers need to internalize the concepts, techniques, and practices to develop a personalized approach to adopting the innovation.

Each teacher has a unique experiential background, including personality and teaching style, that must be addressed during the change process. Learning style-based instruction usually involves a fundamental change of educational philosophy or pedagogy and requires adoption of a new set of teaching tools and practices.

The change process mandates time for reflection, confrontation of resistance (usually centered around classroom-control issues), and introspection regarding revised roles and practices. We discovered that teachers usually begin by adopting those elements with which they identify most strongly, perhaps because the learning styles model is comprehensive.

4. *Implementation:* experimenting with the new concepts, procedures, or techniques.

Implementation involves classroom experimentation with some of the practices inherent in the model. Some teachers begin the implementation stage by redesigning the environment to provide for formal and informal instructional areas. Others begin by varying their grouping arrangements to encourage student involvement in activities or projects alone, in pairs, in small groups, or with the teacher. Others begin by altering how the curriculum is taught so that it responds to students' varied perceptual strengths.

Because implementation involves intensive curriculum redesign and materials and resources development, several years are needed for full-scale change. Certainly this stage involves risk taking when moving from rigid, controlling, content-oriented approaches to flexible, open, student-centered instruction.

5. *Consequences:* focusing on the impact of the change on students, teachers, others, or the system.

The fifth stage in the change process is assessing its initial impact on students. One of the outcomes that should be evident is that students begin to assume a greater responsibility for their own learning and view classroom projects and activities as cooperative rather than competitive tasks.

During our observations, students demonstrated enthusiasm for school, were knowledgeable about their own learning preferences, and gravitated toward those instructional activities that accommodated their styles. Teachers reported a sense of accomplishment and professional renewal.

6. *Collaboration:* sharing, coordinating, and cooperating with other educators toward a specific goal.

Collaboration is critical for implementing change because many secondary school teachers function in relative isolation from their colleagues. Departmental and faculty meetings in large schools frequently focus solely on organizational and administrative concerns and neglect curricular and instructional issues.

If learning styles programs are to be implemented, teachers must meet regularly to share, coordinate, and cooperate with each other. Teachers who are more conversant with the model must function as consultants and support the efforts of those colleagues who are just becoming interested. Teachers must share successes and failures and have the opportunity to observe classrooms in which the changes have been fully implemented. Teachers need to embrace supervision and view it as a means of improving their competence.

7. *Refocusing:* exploring new directions or additional benefits from the change or innovation.

The refocusing stage of planned change involves expanding on the innovation, developing a wider range of materials and resources, and designing new ways to apply the concepts.

For example, one of the recent innovations in learning styles application is teaching secondary school students to bypass the teacher's style, if it is incompatible with their own, by adapting the textbook and developing materials that enhance individual preferences. As the process of change is introduced within the classroom, other applications become obvious.

To illustrate, one principal commented, "I no longer view differences between some faculty members and me as areas of conflict, but perceive them as differences in style. If I can identify their style, I can usually resolve the problem."

Teachers who conduct inservice workshops on learning styles find that their peers respond well when the strategies and techniques used are compatible with their personal adult styles.

8. *Evaluating:* developing a system for assessing the overall impact of the change on students, teachers, and the educational climate.

The final step in the change process is evaluating the effectiveness of the innovation to determine whether it should be sustained or eliminated. Assessment of the impact of learning style-based instruction can take many forms.

Teachers might utilize the case study method with selected students by:

- Keeping anecdotal notes and records about an individual, noting baseline data in behavioral areas such as academic achievement, attendance, time-on-task, attitudes toward school, and so forth
- Observing learning style approaches during a period of time when using techniques that are compatible and incompatible with their students' preferences
- Assessing post-learning style implementation changes and comparing those with baseline data.

Experimental research can be conducted to compare the achievement and/or attitude gains of similarly high IQ groups in classrooms that accommodate students' learning style preferences versus those that do not, or how individuals with specific styles fare in matched and mismatched treatments. Schools that utilize a comprehensive learning styles program also can examine pre and posttest assessments of dropout rates, attendance, self-esteem, and standardized achievement test scores in congruent versus incongruent conditions.

School Change Agents

Kurt Lewin, a noted expert in the change process, observed: "If you want to find out how something works, just try to change it!"

Educators may be convinced of the merits of certain innovations, such as providing for students' learning style preferences, but the process of convincing their colleagues to change existing instructional approaches is very complex.

School change agents exemplify the characteristics of leaders in any organization. They are persistent, energetic, and hard working, risk-taking, goal-directed, adaptable, receptive, and professionally committed. Their credibility with colleagues is high; they are perceived as knowledgeable experts. In addition, they understand the politics and power structure within the school or district and are insightful concerning the change process.

We identified the change agent in each of the 10 schools described in this book. Although 40 percent of the change agents were secondary school principals, others included teachers, assistant directors, and directors. To determine whether common patterns of leadership style and thinking style existed among them, we requested that each of the 10 institutional leaders complete two instruments, the *Styles of Thinking* (Harrison and Bramson, 1982), and the *Administrative Style Inventory* (Dunn and Dunn, 1977).

Styles of Thinking

Harrison and Bramson (1982) postulated that each individual has an idea about a "right" way to think about things. Each individual's preferred strategy has its strengths and weaknesses. Problems arise when a strategy is over-worked, used inappropriately, or when the preferences of others are ignored or disregarded.

The *Styles of Thinking Questionnaire* (Bramson et al., 1980) consists of 18 questions that require the respondent to rank five different responses to each question. The questionnaire uses standard scores and provides inter-pretations ranging from a "very strong preference for this style" to "a neglect of this style." Norming of the scale indicates that managers and administra-tors tend to have the following style preferences.

Style	Percent of Population Preferring Style	General Characteristics
Idealist	37%	Receptive; seeks ideal solu-tions; holistic view; interested in values.
Analyst	35%	Prescriptive; seeks "one best way"; logical; interested in scientific solutions.
Realist	24%	Empirical; relies on facts and expert opinion; seeks solu-tions that meet current needs; interested in concrete results.
Pragmatist	18%	Eclectic; adaptive; seeks short-est route to payoff; interested in innovation.
Synthesist	11%	Integrative; speculative; seeks conflict and synthesis; inter-ested in change.

These percentages total 125 because some respondents had two or more style preferences. A description of each of the five thinking styles, together with their strengths and liabilities, is included in the table on page 64.

An analysis of the learning style catalysts in the schools we visited revealed the following thinking style preferences:

Rank	Style	Percent of Leaders Preferring
1	Idealist	62%
2	Pragmatist	57%
3	Analyst	14%
4	Synthesist	14%
5	Realist	0%

Again, these percentages total 147 because some respondents had two style preferences.

Overall, the catalysts differed significantly from the normed groups concerning their style rankings and strength of preferences. The catalysts can best be described as idealistic pragmatists; that is, persons who are receptive, open, goal-directed, and adaptive with an interest in ideal solutions and pragmatic results.

School Administrators' Management Style

A second instrument was used to assess the managerial styles of school administrators (Dunn and Dunn, 1977). Individual administrators may function in a variety of styles, depending on the administrative task or the faculty with whom they are interacting. For example, an administrator may function collaboratively in the area of educational planning and operate autocratically in areas of management and control.

That same administrator may function either collaboratively or in a laissez-faire manner with a teacher who is respected, but autocratically with one who has not lived up to his or her expectations. That same administrator may also function as a benevolent despot when an issue of morality or values develops.

The seven styles measured on this scale, from low to high administrative control, are:

1. Collaborative
2. Cooperative
3. Participative
4. Bureaucratic
5. Laissez-faire
6. Benevolent despot
7. Autocratic

An analysis of the management style of the catalysts in the schools we visited revealed the following preferences:

Rank	Style	Raw Scores*
1.	Collaborative	64
2.	Benevolent Despot	105
3.	Participative	112
4.	Cooperative	120
5.	Autocratic	156
6.	Bureaucratic	169
7.	Laissez-faire	170

A clear pattern seems to have emerged among our catalysts. The preferred style is collaborative, followed by benevolent despot, and a general rejection of middle-of-the-road approaches, including bureaucratic and laissez-faire.

Collaboration is the highest level of democratic administration, reflecting a responsiveness and cohesive rapport between an administrator and all individuals and groups. Teachers, counselors, supervisors, and administrators work together on objectives, plans, procedures, evaluations, and redesigns. Delegation of authority is made more and more to groups; ownership of responsibility is assumed by all members.

The secondary management style of our catalysts is that of the benevolent despot who usually smiles, puts a proverbial arm around the shoulder of a colleague while listening, and then directs or does as she or he believes "best." Input and involvement are either accidental and a function of a predetermined decision, or solicited to ensure results as previously projected by the catalyst.

The style most strongly denounced by the catalysts in the secondary schools we visited is laissez-faire, which suggests a chaotic, permissive

---

*The lowest scores reveal the strongest preference because statements related to operation of building or program, handbooks, crisis reaction, and planning are rank ordered from 1 to 7 with No. 1 being the statement most liked by the respondent and 7 the least liked.

approach characterized by the educator who buries his or her head in the sand of the organization on a regular basis, allowing staff members to do their own thing.

Summary

The catalysts who initiated the quiet revolution in the secondary schools we visited held a variety of positions, ranging from classroom teacher to K-12 director. However, most frequently, they were secondary school principals who perceived their major role to be the instructional leader.

Their leadership styles were idealistic, pragmatic, and collaborative. They were persons of high credibility, persistence, and status, perceived by teachers as knowledgeable and expert in the area of instructional methods and techniques. They were astute concerning the *process* of change and involved the most effective persons available in moving toward learning styles-based instruction.

In addition, these catalysts actively and personally participated in in-service training with faculty members by attending workshops, institutes, and seminars and, afterward, often conducted similar sessions for their colleagues and demonstrated specific learning styles strategies which they had adopted.

Epilog

Although the drive, direction, and strategies for implementing learning styles emanated from different sources and were channeled differently by the leaders we described in this book, they did have certain common characteristics.

- They each had become knowledgeable about learning styles. They had learned enough about the concept and its practical applications to actively participate in sharing information with and teaching their colleagues. Thus, they were able to encourage others to participate in the movement and to provide a support system for them.
- They each had excellent management skills. Their techniques differed, but all of them knew how to focus on what they wanted to achieve and how to manage their time and energies to permit active involvement in the change process.
- They each had vision, commitment, energy, and persistence to move their educational communities toward more effective instruction. They knew they could change the system and they channeled everyone and everything around them into the direction in which they believed their schools should move.

NASSP Executive Director Scott Thomson described the components of leadership as: knowledge of the business of education; possession and exercise of management skills; and the vision and energy to move faculty and students toward more effective schooling.[1] We believe that is what it takes to improve the system.

We would like to return to each of these sites three years from now to see what changes have occurred and how teachers, students, administrators, and parents are reacting.

Perhaps this book has triggered your interest sufficiently to become involved with learning styles. We would like you to see for yourself the quiet revolution we observed in the secondary schools we visited.

---

1. Scott D. Thomson, "Focus on Leadership." *NASSP NewsLeader,* September 1987.

APPENDIX A

References

Bentzen, M.M. *Changing Schools: The Magic Feather Principle.* New York: McGraw-Hill, 1974.

Bloom, B.S. *Stability and Change in Human Characteristics.* New York: Wiley & Sons, 1964.

Bok, D. *Higher Learning.* Cambridge, Mass.: Harvard University Press, 1986.

Boyer, E.L. "Early Schooling and the Nation's Future." *Educational Leadership* 44(1987):4-8.

Bramson, R.M.; Parlette, A.; Harrison, A.F.; and Associates. *InQ: Preference in Ways of Asking Questions and Making Decisions.* Berkeley, Calif.: University of California, 1980.

Cafferty, E.I. "An Analysis of Student Performance Based Upon the Degree of Match Between the Educational Cognitive Style of the Teachers and the Educational Cognitive Style of the Students." Doctoral dissertation, University of Nebraska, 1980. *Dissertation Abstracts International* 41(1980):2908A.

Carbo, M. "An Analysis of the Relationship Between the Modality Preferences of Kindergartners and Selected Reading Treatments as They Affect the Learning of a Basic Sight-Word Vocabulary." Doctoral dissertation, St. John's University, New York. *Dissertation Abstracts International* 41(1980):1389-04A.

Carbo, M.; Dunn, R.; and Dunn, K. *Teaching Students To Read Through Their Individual Learning Styles.* Englewood Cliffs, N.J.: Prentice-Hall, 1986.

Carruthers, S.A., and Young, L.A. "Preference of Condition Concerning Time in Learning Environments of Rural Versus City Eighth Grade Students." *Learning Styles NETWORK Newsletter,* Spring 1980.

Cholakis, M.A. "An Experimental Investigation of the Relationships Between and Among Sociological Preferences, Vocabulary Instruction and Achievement, and the Attitudes of New York, Urban, Seventh and Eighth Grade Underachievers." Doctoral dissertation, St. John's University, New York. *Dissertation Abstracts International* 47(1986):11 4046-A.

Clay, J.E. "A Correlational Analysis of the Learning Characteristics of Highly Achieving and Poorly Achieving Freshmen at A&M University as Revealed Through Performance on Standardized Tests." Normal, Ala.: Alabama A&M University, 1984.

Cody, C. "Learning Styles, Including Hemispheric Dominance: A Comparative Study of Average, Gifted and Highly Gifted Students in Grades Five Through Twelve." Doctoral dissertation, Temple University. *Dissertation Abstracts International* 44(1983):1631-6A.

Cohen, L. "Birth Order and Learning Styles: An Examination of the Relationships Between Birth Order and Middle School Students' Preferred Learning Style Profile." Doctoral dissertation, University of Minnesota's Graduate Department of Educational Psychology, 1986.

Cone, W.H. "Brain Research Findings May Improve Decision Making." *NASSP Bulletin,* February 1982.

Copenhaver, R. "The Consistency of Student Learning Styles as Students Move from English to Mathematics." Doctoral dissertation, Indiana University, 1979. *Dissertation Abstracts International* 40(1979):3735A.

Crino, E.M. "An Analysis of the Preferred Learning Styles of Kindergarten Children and the Relationship of These Preferred Learning Styles to Curriculum Planning for Kindergarten Children." Doctoral dissertation, State University of New York, Buffalo, 1984. *Dissertation Abstracts International* 45/05(1984):1282A.

Cross, J.A., Jr. "Prevalence in Internal Locus of Control in Artistically Talented Students." Research Study, University of Alabama, 1982.

Cupke, L.F. "The Effects of Similarity of Instructor Preferred Teaching Style and Student Preferred Learning Style on Student Achievement in Selected Courses in a Metropolitan Community College." Doctoral dissertation, University of Missouri-Kansas City. *Dissertation Abstracts International* 41(1980):988-03A.

Curry, L. *Integrating Concepts of Cognitive or Learning Styles: A Review with Attention to Psychometric Standards.* Ottawa, Ontario: Canadian College of Health Services Executives, 1987.

DeBello, T. "A Critical Analysis of the Achievement and Attitude Effects of Administrative Assignments to Social Studies Writing Instruction Based on Identified, Eighth Grade Students' Learning Style Preferences for Learning Alone, with Peers, or with Teachers." Doctoral dissertation, St. John's University, New York. *Dissertation Abstracts International* 47(1985):68-01A.

Decker, B.C. "Cultural Diversity, Another Element To Recognize in Learning Style." *NASSP Bulletin,* September 1983.

Della Valle, J. "An Experimental Investigation of the Relationship(s) Between Preference for Mobility and the Word Recognition Scores of Seventh Grade Students To Provide Supervisory and Administrative Guidelines for the Organization of Effective Instructional Environments." Doctoral dissertation, St. John's University, New York. *Dissertation Abstracts International* 45(1984):359-02A.

Domino, G. "Interactive Effects of Achievement Orientation and Teaching Style on Academic Achievement." *ACT Research Report* 39(1970):1-9.

Douglass, C.B. "Making Biology Easier To Understand." *The American Biology Teacher* 41(1979):277-279.

Dunn, R. "Teaching in a Purple Fog: What We Don't Know About Learning Style." *NASSP Bulletin,* March 1981.

Dunn, R., and Bruno, A. "What Does the Research on Learning Styles Have To Do with Mario?" *The Clearing House* 1(1985):9-11.

Dunn, R., and Dunn, K. Administrative Style Inventory. In *Administrator's Guide to New Programs for Faculty Management and Evaluation.* West Nyack, N.Y.: Parker Publishing, 1977.

———. Teaching Style Inventory. In *Administrator's Guide to New Programs for Faculty Management and Evaluation.* Englewood Cliffs, N.J.: Prentice-Hall, 1977.

Dunn, R., and Price, G. "Identifying the Learning Style Characteristics of Gifted Children." *Gifted Child Quarterly* 1(1980):33-36.

Dunn, R.; Cavanaugh, D.; Eberle, B.; and Zenhausern, R. "Hemispheric Preference: The Newest Element of Learning Style." *The American Biology Teacher* 5(1982):291-294.

Dunn, R.; Della Valle, J.; Dunn, K.; Geisert, G.; Sinatra, R.; and Zenhausern, R. "The Effects of Matching and Mismatching Students' Mobility Preferences on Recognition and Memory Tasks." *Journal of Educational Research* 5(1986):267-272.

Dunn, R.; Dunn, K.; and Freeley, M.E. "Tips To Improve Your In-Service Training." *Early Years,* April 1985.

Dunn, R.; Dunn, K.; and Freeley, M.E. "Practical Applications of the Research: Responding to Students; Learning Styles-Step One." *Illinois State Research and Development Journal* 1(1984):1-21.

Dunn, R.; Pizzo, J.; Sinatra, R.; and Barreto, R.A. "Can It Be Too Quiet To Learn?" *Focus: Teaching English Language Arts,* Winter 1983, pp. 2-22.

Dunn, R.; White, R.M.; and Zenhausern, R. "An Investigation of Responsible Versus Less Responsible Students." *Illinois Association of Supervision and Curriculum Development* 19(1):19-24.

Fantini, M. *Regaining Excellence in Education.* Columbus, Ohio: Merrill Publishing Co., 1986.

Fantini, M., and Weinstein, G. *The Disadvantaged: Challenge to Education.* New York: Harper and Row, 1968.

Farr, B.J. "Individual Differences in Learning: Predicting One's More Effective Learning Modality." Doctoral dissertation, Catholic University, 1971. *Dissertation Abstracts International* 32(1971):1332A.

Freeley, M.E. "An Experimental Investigation of the Relationships Among Teachers' Individual Time Preferences, Inservice Workshop Schedules, and Instructional Techniques and the Subsequent Implementation of Learning Style Strategies in Participants' Classrooms." Doctoral dissertation, St. John's University, New York. *Dissertation Abstracts International* 46(1984):403-02A.

Gadwa, K., and Griggs, S.A. "The School Dropout: Implications for Counselors." *The School Counselor* 33(1985):9-17.

Gadwa, K.; Christensen, J.; Bryan, E.; and Boeck, D. "School Dropout Study—A Final Report." Lynwood, Wash.: Edmonds School District, 1983.

Gardiner, B. "An Experimental Analysis of Selected Teaching Strategies Implemented at Specific Times of the School Day and Their Effects on the Social Studies Achievement Test Scores and Attitudes of Fourth-Grade Low-Achieving Students in an Urban School Setting." Doctoral dissertation, St. John's University, New York, 1986.

Giunta, S.F. "Administrative Considerations Concerning Learning Style, Its Relationship to Teaching Style, and the Influence of Instructor/Student Congruence on High Schoolers." Dissertation, St. John's University, New York. *Dissertation Abstracts International* 45(1984):32-01A.

Goodlad, J.I. *A Place Called School: Prospects for the Future.* New York: McGraw-Hill, 1984.

Gould, B.J. "An Investigation of the Relationships Between Supervisors and Supervisees' Sociological Productivity Styles on Teacher Evaluations and Interpersonal Attraction Ratings." Doctoral dissertation, St. John's University, New York, 1987.

Griggs, S. "A Diagnostic Process: Counseling for Individual Learning Style." *NASSP Bulletin,* October 1981.

Griggs, S. and Price, G. "A Comparison Between the Learning Styles of Gifted Versus Average Suburban Junior High School Students." *Roeper Review* 3(1980):7-9.

Harrison, A.F., and Bramson, R.M. *Styles of Thinking.* Garden City, N.Y.: Anchor/Doubleday, 1982.

Heikkinen, M.; Pettigrew, F.; and Zakrajsek, D. "Learning Styles vs. Teaching Styles—Studying the Relationship." *NASSP Bulletin,* February 1985.

Hodges, H. "An Analysis of the Relationships Among Preferences for a Formal/Informal Design, One Element of Learning Style, Academic Achievement, and Attitudes of Seventh and Eighth Grade Students in Remedial Mathematics Classes in a New York City Junior High School." Doctoral dissertation, St. John's University, New York. *Dissertation Abstracts International* 45(1985):2791A.

Holt, J. *What Do I Do Monday?* New York: E.P. Dutton, 1970.

Jacobs, R.L. "The Classification and Comparison of Learning Style Preferences of Selected Groups of Students According to Race and Achievement Levels." Doctoral dissertation, George Peabody College for Teachers of Vanderbilt University, 1987.

Jalali, F. "A Cross Cultural Comparative Analysis of the Learning Style and Field Dependence/Independence Characteristics of Selected Afro-American, Chinese, Greek, and Mexican American Junior High School Students." Doctoral dissertation, St. John's University, in press.

Jarsonbeck, S. "The Effects of a Right-Brain and Mathematics Curriculum on Low Achieving, Fourth Grade Students." Doctoral dissertation, University of South Florida. *Dissertation Abstracts International* 45(1984):2791A.

Johnson, C.D. "Identifying Potential School Dropouts." Doctoral dissertation, United States International University. *Dissertation Abstracts International* 45(1984):2397A.

Kaley, S.B. "Field Dependence/Independence and Learning Styles in Sixth Graders." Doctoral dissertation, Hofstra University. *Dissertation Abstracts International* 38(1977):3A 1301.

Kettner, P.; Daley, J.M.; and Nichols, A.W. *Initiating Change in Organizations and Communities.* Monterey, Calif.: Brooks/Cole, 1985.

Kintsch, W. "Concerning the Marriage of Research and Practice in Beginning Reading Instruction." In *Theory and Practice of Early Reading,* edited by L.B. Resnick and P.A. Weaver. Hillsdale, N.J.: Lawrence Erlbaum Associates, 1979.

Kohl, H.R. *The Open Classroom.* New York: The New York Review, 1969.

Kreitner, K.R. "Modality Strengths and Learning Styles of Musically Talented High School Students." Master's thesis, Ohio State University, 1981.

Krimsky, J. "A Comparative Analysis of the Effects of Matching and Mismatching Fourth Grade Students with Their Learning Style Preference for the Environmental Element of Light and Their Subsequent Reading Speed and Accuracy Scores." Doctoral dissertation, St. John's University, New York. *Dissertation Abstracts International* 43(1982):66-01A.

Kroon, D. "An Experimental Investigation of the Effects on Academic Achievement and the Resultant Administrative Implications and Instruction Congruent and Incongruent with Secondary, Industrial Arts Students' Learning Style Perceptual Preferences." Doctoral dissertation, St. John's University, New York. *Dissertation Abstracts International* 46(1985):3247A.

Kulp, J.J. "A Description of the Processes Used in Developing and Implementing a Teacher Training Program Based on Dunns' Concept of Learning Style." Doctoral dissertation, Temple University. *Dissertation Abstracts International* 42(1982):5021A.

Lam-Phoon, S. "A Comparative Study of the Learning Styles of Southeast Asian and American Caucasian College Students of Two Seventh-Day Adventist Campuses." Doctoral dissertation, Andrews University, Michigan, 1986.

LeClair, T.J. "The Preferred Modality of Kindergarten-Aged Children." Master of Arts thesis, California State University, Long Beach, 1986.

Lemmon, P. "A School Where Learning Styles Makes a Difference." *Principal,* March 1985, pp. 26-29.

Lengel, O. "Analysis of the Preferred Learning Styles of Former Adolescent Psychiatric Patients." Doctoral dissertation, Kansas State University. *Dissertation Abstracts International* 44(1983):08 2344-A.

Lerner, B. "Vouchers for Literacy: Second Chance Legislation." *Phi Delta Kappan* 62(1981):252-255.

Lynch, P.K. "An Analysis of the Relationships Among Academic Achievement, Attendance, and the Learning Style Time Preferences of Eleventh and Twelfth Grade Students Identified as Initial or Chronic Truants in a Suburban New York School District." Doctoral dissertation, St. John's University, New York. *Dissertation Abstracts International* 42(1981):1880A.

MacMurren, H. "A Comparative Study of the Effects of Matching and Mismatching Sixth-Grade Students with Their Learning Style Preferences for the Physical Element of Intake and Their Subsequent Reading Speed and Accuracy Scores and Attitudes." Doctoral dissertation, St John's University, New York. *Dissertation Abstracts International* 46(1985):3247A.

McEwen, P. "Learning Styles, Intelligence, and Creativity Among Elementary School Students." Master's thesis, State University, College at Buffalo (Center for Studies on Creativity), 1985.

Maeroff, G.L. "Rule Tying Promotion to Reading Skill Stirs Worry." *New York Times,* April 3, 1982.

Mariash, L.J. "Identification of Characteristics of Learning Styles Existent Among Students Attending School in Selected Northeastern Manitoba Communities." Master's thesis, University of Manitoba, Winnipeg, Manitoba, 1983.

Martin, M.A. "Cognitive Styles and Their Implications for Computer-Based Instruction." *Journal of Computer-Based Instruction,* May 1983, pp. 241-244.

Martin, M.K. "Effects of the Interaction Between Students' Learning Styles and High School Instructional Environments." Doctoral dissertation, University of Oregon, 1977.

Martini, M. "An Analysis of the Relationships Between and Among Computer-Assisted Instruction, Learning Style Perceptual Preferences, Attitudes, and the Science Achievement of Seventh Grade Students in a Suburban, New York School District." Doctoral dissertation, St. John's University, New York. *Dissertation Abstracts International* 47(1986):877-03A.

Messer, P.L. "Building Usage and Learning Styles at the Middle Level." *NASSP Bulletin,* May 1983.

Miles, B. "An Investigation of the Relationships Among the Learning Style Sociological Preferences of Fifth and Sixth Grade Students, Selected Interactive Classroom Patterns, and Achievement in Career Awareness and Career Decision-Making Concepts." Doctoral dissertation, St. John's University, New York, 1987.

Miller, L.M. "Mobility as an Element of Learning Style: The Effect Its Inclusion or Exclusion Has on Student Performance in the Standardized Testing Environment." Master's thesis, University of North Florida, 1985.

Millerick, W. "Compensating for the Cognitive Differences of Individual Learners Enrolled in the Various Academic Disciplines Within a Business School Curriculum." *Journal of Computer-Based Instruction,* May 1983, pp. 144-151.

Morgan, H.L. "Learning Styles: The Relationship Between Need for Structure and Preferred Mode of Instruction for Gifted Elementary Students." Doctoral dissertation, University of Pittsburgh, 1981.

Morris, V.J.P. "The Design and Implementation of a Teaching Strategy for Language Arts at Chipley High School That Brings About Predictable Learning Outcomes." Doctoral dissertation, Florida State University. *Dissertation Abstracts International* 44(1983):3231-A.

Murrain, P.G. "Administrative Determinations Concerning Facilities Utilization and Instructional Grouping: An Analysis of the Relationship(s) Between Selected Thermal Environments and Preferences for Temperature, an Element of Learning Style, as They Affect Word Recognition Scores of Secondary Students." Doctoral dissertation, St. John's University, New York. *Dissertation Abstracts International* 44(1983):1749-06A.

Murray, C.A. "The Comparison of Learning Styles Between Low and High Reading Achievement Subjects in the Seventh and Eighth Grades in a Public Middle School." Doctoral dissertation, United States International University. *Dissertation Abstracts International* 41(1980):03A 1005.

Napolitano, R.A. "An Experimental Investigation of the Relationships Among Achievement, Attitude Scores, and Traditionally, Marginally, and Underprepared College Students Enrolled in an Introductory Psychology Course When They Are Matched and Mismatched with Their Learning Style Preferences for the Element of Structure." Doctoral dissertation, St. John's University, New York. *Dissertation Abstracts International* 47(1986):02 435-A.

Patterson, Sheri. "A Dean of Students Uses Learning Styles." *Learning Style NET-WORK Newsletter* 8(1986):5.

Pederson, J.K. "The Classification and Comparison of Learning Style Preferences of Learning Disabled Students and Gifted Students." Doctoral dissertation, Texas Tech University, 1984. *Dissertation Abstracts International* 46(1984):342-02A.

Piatt, J.G. "Brain Processing Preferences: Key to an Organization's Success." *NASSP Bulletin,* December 1983.

Pizzo, J. "An Investigation of the Relationships Between Selected Acoustic Environments and Sound, an Element of Learning Style, as They Affect Sixth Grade Students' Reading Achievement and Attitudes." Doctoral dissertation, St. John's University, New York. *Dissertation Abstracts International* 42(1981):2475A.

————. "Breaking the Sound Barrier: Classroom Noise and Learning Style." *Set. Research Information for Teachers.* New Zealand: New Zealand Council for Educational Research 2, 1983.

Price, G. "Which Learning Style Elements Are Stable and Which Tend To Change?" *Learning Styles NETWORK Newsletter* 3(1980):1.

Price, G.; Dunn, R.; and Sanders, W. "Reading Achievement and Learning Style Characteristics." *The Clearing House* 5(1981):223-226.

Ramirez, A.I. "Modality and Field Dependence/Independence: Learning Components and Their Relationship to Mathematics Achievement in the Elementary School." Doctoral dissertation, Florida State University. *Dissertation Abstracts International* 43(1982):03A-666.

Raywid, M. "The First Decade of Public School Alternatives." *Early Years,* November 1981, pp. 17-18.

Reabe, L. "Learning Styles Brought Amazing Gains to My High School Underachieving Students!" *Learning Styles NETWORK Newsletter,* Summer 1986.

Renzi, N.B. "A Study of Some Effects of Field Dependence-Independence and Feedback on Performance Achievement." Doctoral dissertation, Hofstra University, 1974. *Dissertation Abstracts International* 35(1974):2059A.

Restak, R. *The Brain: The Last Frontier.* New York: Doubleday, 1979.

Ricca, J. "Curricular Implications of Learning Style Differences Between Gifted and Non-Gifted Students." Doctoral dissertation, State University of New York at Buffalo. *Dissertation Abstracts International* 44(1983):05 1324-A.

Ritt, B., and Gomery, J. "Learning Styles and Staff Development: A Combination for Effective Learning." *NASSP Bulletin,* March 1987.

Roberts, O.A. "Investigation of the Relationship Between Learning Style and Temperament of Senior High School Students in the Bahamas and Jamaica." Graduate dissertation, Andrews University, 1984.

Rogers, V. *Teaching in the British Primary School.* New York: Macmillan, 1970.

Schmeck, R.; Ribich, F.; and Ramanaiah, N. "Development of a Self-Report Inventory for Assessing Individual Differences in Learning Processes." *Applied Psychological Measurement* 1(1977).

Schwen, T.M. "The Effect of Cognitive Styles and Instructional Sequences on Learning on Hierarchical Task." Doctoral dissertation, Indiana University. *Dissertation Abstracts International* 31(1970):2797A-2798A.

Shea, T.C. "An Investigation of the Relationship Among Preferences for the Learning Style Element of Design, Selected Instructional Environments, and Reading Achievement with Ninth Grade Students To Improve Administrative Determinations Concerning Effective Educational Facilities." Doctoral dissertation, St. John's University, New York. *Dissertation Abstracts International* 44(1983):2004-07A.

Siebenman, J.B. "An Investigation of the Relationship Between Learning Style and Cognitive Style in Non-Traditional College Reading Students." Doctoral dissertation, Arizona State University. *Dissertation Abstracts International* 45(1984):1705-06A.

Sinatra, R.; Primavera, L.; and Waked, W.J. "Learning Styles and Intelligence of Reading Disabled Students." *Perceptual and Motor Skills* 62(1986):1243-1250.

Spires, R.D. "The Effect of Teacher Inservice About Learning Styles on Students' Mathematics and Reading Achievement." Doctoral dissertation, Bowling Green State University. *Dissertation Abstracts International* 44(1983):05 1325A.

Steinauer, M.H. "Interpersonal Relationships as Reflected in Learning Style Preferences: A Study of Eleventh Grade Students and Their English Teachers in a Vocational School." Doctoral dissertation, Southern Illinois University. *Dissertation Abstracts International* 43(1981):305-02A.

Stewart, E.D. "Learning Styles Among Gifted/Talented Students: Instructional Technique Preferences." *Exceptional Children* 48(1981):134-138.

Stiles, R. "Learning Style Preferences for Design and Their Relationship to Standardized Test Results." Doctoral dissertation, The University of Tennessee. *Dissertation Abstracts International* 46(1985):Order No. DA 8524144.

Tanenbaum, R. "An Investigation of the Relationships Between Selected Instructional Techniques and Identified Field Dependent and Field Independent Cognitive Styles as Evidenced Among High School Students Enrolled in Studies of Nutrition." Doctoral dissertation, St. John's University, New York. *Dissertation Abstracts International* 43(1982):68-01A.

Tappenden, V.J. "Analysis of the Learning Styles of Vocational Education and Non-vocational Education Students in Eleventh and Twelfth Grades from Rural, Urban, and Suburban Locations in Ohio." Doctoral dissertation, Kent State University. *Dissertation Abstracts International* 44(1983):1326A.

Thies, A. "A Brain Behavior Analysis of Learning Style." In *Student Learning Styles: Diagnosing and Prescribing Programs.* Reston, Va.: NASSP, 1979.

Thrasher, R. *A Study of the Learning Style Preferences of At-Risk Sixth and Ninth-Grade Students.* Pompano Beach, Fla.: Florida Association of Alternative School Educators, 1985.

Trautman, P. "An Investigation of the Relationship Between Selected Instructional Techniques and Identified Cognitive Style." Doctoral dissertation, St. John's University, New York. *Dissertation Abstracts International* 43(1979):68-01A.

Urbschat, K. "A Study of Preferred Learning Modes and Their Relationship to the Amount of Recall of CVC Trigrams." Doctoral dissertation, Wayne State University. *Dissertation Abstracts International* 38(1977):2536-5A.

Vignia, R.A. "An Investigation of Learning Styles of Gifted and Non-Gifted High School Students." Doctoral dissertation, University of Houston, 1983.

Virostko, J. "An Analysis of the Relationships Among Academic Achievement in Mathematics and Reading, Assigned Instructional Schedules, and the Learning Style Time Preferences of Third, Fourth, Fifth, and Sixth Grade Students." Doctoral dissertation, St. John's University, New York. *Dissertation Abstracts International* 44(1983):1683-06A.

Wasson, F.R. "A Comparative Analysis of Learning Styles and Personality Characteristics of Achieving and Underachieving Gifted Elementary Students." Doctoral dissertation, Florida State University. *Dissertation Abstracts International* 41(1980):3933A.

Weinberg, F. "An Experimental Investigation of the Interaction Between Sensory Modality Preference and Mode of Presentation in the Instruction of Arithmetic Concepts to Third Grade Underachievers." *Dissertation Abstracts International* 44(1983):1740-06A.

Wheeler, R. "An Investigation of the Degree of Academic Achievement Evidenced When Second Grade, Learning Disabled Students' Perceptual Preferences Are

Matched and Mismatched with Complementary Sensory Approaches To Beginning Reading Instruction." Doctoral dissertation, St. John's University, New York. *Dissertation Abstracts International* 44(1983):2039-07A.

White, R. "An Investigation of the Relationship Between Selected Instructional Methods and Selected Elements of Emotional Learning Style upon Student Achievement in Seventh Grade Social Studies." Doctoral dissertation, St. John's University, New York. *Dissertation Abstracts International* 42(1980):995-03A.

Wild, J.B. "A Study of the Learning Styles of Learning Disabled Students and Non-Learning Disabled Students at the Junior High School Level." Master's thesis, University of Kansas, Lawrence, 1979.

Williams, G.L. "The Effectiveness of Computer-Assisted Instruction and Its Relationship to Selected Learning Style Elements." Doctoral dissertation, North Texas State University. *Dissertation Abstracts International* 45(1984):1986A.

Wingo, L.H. "Relationships Among Locus of Motivation, Sensory Modality and Grouping Preferences of Learning Style to Basic Skills Test Performance in Reading and Mathematics." Doctoral dissertation, Memphis State University. *Dissertation Abstracts International* 41(1980):07A 2923.

Wittig, C. "Learning Style Preferences Among Students High or Low on Divergent Thinking and Feeling Variables." Master's thesis, State University College of Buffalo, New York (Center for Studies in Creativity), 1985.

Wolfe, G. "Learning Styles and the Teaching of Reading." Doctoral dissertation, Akron University. *Dissertation Abstracts International* 45(1983):3422A.

Annotated Bibliography of Key Publications on Learning Styles

A Review of Articles and Books. Jamaica, N.Y.: The Center for the Study of Learning and Teaching Styles, St. John's University, 1987, 260 pp.

Contains approximately 65 articles on learning styles and brain behavior reprinted from major journals.

Annotated Bibliography. Jamaica, N.Y.: Learning Styles NETWORK cosponsored by the National Association of Secondary School Principals and St. John's University, 1987.

This updated review of articles, books, dissertations, and research on learning styles is the dream-come-true of persons involved in either research or term paper reviews.

Carbo, M.; Dunn, R.; and Dunn, K. *Teaching Students To Read Through Their Individual Learning Styles.* Englewood Cliffs, N.J.: Prentice-Hall, 1986, 307 pp.

This text provides practical, classroom-tested models and examples that can be used to promote a love of reading and reading efficiency at any level. It details specific techniques, and accompanies explanations with sequential, easy-to-follow recommendations for designing and using the techniques in any class or Resource Room.

Della Valle, J.; Dunn, K.; Dunn, R.; Geisert, G.; Sinatra, R.; and Zenhausern, R. "The Effects of Matching and Mismatching Students' Mobility Preferences on Recognition and Memory Tasks." *Journal of Educational Research* 79(1986):267-272.

This article abstracts an experimental research study that measured the effects of matching and mismatching students' mobility preferences on recognition and memory tasks.

Dunn, K. "Madison Prep: Alternative to Teenage Disaster." *Educational Leadership* 38(1981):386-387.

Describes an alternative school in New York City that made successful use of individual learning styles.

Dunn, K., and Dunn, R. "Dispelling Outmoded Beliefs About Student Learning." *Educational Leadership* 44(1987):55-61.

This article identifies 15 popular fallacious beliefs regarding learning and discusses the research that refutes these myths, citing learning style accommodation as the key to learning enhancement.

Dunn, R. "Learning Styles: Link Between Individual Differences and Effective Instruction." *Educational Leadership* 2(1986):3-22.

This article defines learning styles and abstracts a large number of award-winning research studies that indicate higher student achievement and improved attitudes result when individual styles are accommodated through complementary instructional strategies.

————. "Research on Instructional Environments: Implications for Student Achievement and Attitudes." *Professional School Psychology* 2(1987):43-52.

Children tend to obtain significantly higher achievement test scores and report

Dunn, R., and Cole, R.W. "Inviting Malpractice Through Mainstreaming." *Educational Leadership* 36(1979):302-306.

Mainstreaming handicapped students without providing adequately for their special needs is malpractice and may lead to litigation.

Dunn, R.; DeBello, T.; Brennan, P.; and Murrain, P. "Learning Style Researchers Define Differences Differently." *Educational Leadership* 38 (1981):372-375.

This article defines eight major theoretical approaches to learning styles and reviews the instruments and instructional applications of each theory.

————. *Teaching Students Through Their Individual Learning Styles: A Practical Approach.* Reston, Va.: Reston Publishing Co., 1978, 431 pp.

This practical guide translates learning style theory into techniques that can be used in the classroom. Readers learn how to identify the individual learning styles, how to teach students with different learning styles, and how to set up the classroom to physically accommodate these individualized styles.

————. "Ten Ways To Make the Classroom a Better Place To Learn." *Instructor* 94(1984):84-88, 139.

The authors identify 10 myths concerning how students learn, cite the research that refutes these myths, and suggest improved practices to enhance learning.

————. "Principals as Instructional Leaders." *Momentum* 17(1986):28-32.

Research is presented that challenges 12 popular high school conventions.

Dunn, R.; Dunn, K.; Primavera, L.; Sinatra, R.; and Virostko, J. "A Timely Solution: Effects of Chronobiology on Achievement and Behavior." *The Clearing House* 61(1987):5-8.

This article describes award-winning research, which reveals the statistically higher achievement in reading and mathematics of students in grades 3 to 6 when they are taught over a two-year period during their learning style time preference.

Dunn, R.; Krimsky, J.S.; Murray, J.B.; and Quinn, P.J. "Light Up Their Lives: A Review of Research on the Effects of Lighting on Children's Achievement and Behavior." *The Reading Teacher* 38(1985):863-869.

Some children have strong preferences for either bright or dim lighting. Accommodating their preferences may profoundly influence their school achievement.

Griggs, S.A. "Counseling the Gifted and Talented Based on Learning Styles." *Exceptional Children* 50(1984):429-432.

Research studies have identified a core of learning style preferences among gifted and talented students, which suggests that they are independent learners, internally controlled, persistent, and perceptually strong.

————. *Counseling Students Through Their Individual Learning Styles.* Ann Arbor, Mich.: ERIC Counseling and Personnel Services Clearinghouse, 1985, 103 pp.

The counseling model begins with an assessment of individual needs and identifies a wide variety of techniques that are compatible with those individual learning style preferences. A variety of counseling techniques, appropriate for students in grades 1 to 12, are described and analyzed.

Keefe, J.W. *Learning Style: Theory and Practice*. Reston, Va.: National Association of Secondary School Principals, 1987, 48 pp.

This pamphlet presents an overview of the cognitive, affective, and physiological characteristics of learning styles. Keefe describes a variety of comprehensive instruments that identify individual style and brain behavior and discusses schoolwide and classroom applications.

National Association of Secondary School Principals. *Student Learning Styles and Brain Behavior*. Reston, Va.: NASSP, 1982, 232 pp.

The format of this volume emulates the threefold thrust of the first major conference for practitioners and researchers on student learning styles and brain behavior programs, instrumentation, and research.

————. *Student Learning Styles: Diagnosing and Prescribing Programs*. Reston, Va.: NASSP, 1979, 137 pp.

This volume describes the pioneering work in student learning style. It reports upon the research base as well as the experience of practitioners in secondary schools working with learning styles.

The Learning Styles NETWORK Newsletter. Jamaica, N.Y.: Learning Styles NETWORK cosponsored by the National Association of Secondary School Principals and St. John's University.

This publication reports on the most recent research, school programs, and manuscripts concerning learning styles and provides practical, how-to suggestions for implementation. Three issues were published in each of nine years (1979-1987) and are available at $3 per issue or $84 for all 27 issues.